Cakes and
Bakes

Cakes and
Bakes

Over 70 recipes for
delicious homemade bakes

hamlyn

A Pyramid Paperback

First published in Great Britain in 2007 by Hamlyn,
a division of Octopus Publishing Group Ltd,
2–4 Heron Quays, London E14 4JP

ISBN-13: 978-0-600-61604-7
ISBN-10: 0-600-61604-5

A CIP catalogue record for this book is available from the
British Library

Printed and bound in China

10 9 8 7 6 5 4 3 2 1

Notes

Both metric and imperial measurements have been
given in all recipes. Use one set of measurements only,
and not a mixture of both.

Standard level spoon measurements are used in all recipes.
1 tablespoon = one 15 ml spoon
1 teaspoon = one 5 ml spoon

Ovens should be preheated to the specified temperature
If using a fan-assisted oven, follow the manufacturer's
instructions for adjusting the time and the temperature.

Medium eggs should be used unless otherwise stated.

This book includes dishes made with nuts and nut
derivatives. It is advisable for those with known allergic
reactions to nuts and nut derivatives and those who may
be potentially vulnerable to these allergies, such as
pregnant and nursing mothers, invalids, the elderly, babies
and children to avoid dishes made with nuts and nut oils.
It is also prudent to check the labels of pre-prepared
ingredients for the possible inclusion of nut derivatives.

The recipes in this book were originally published in the
following Hamlyn titles: *30 Minute Vegetarian, Cake,
Chocolate, Citrus, Cupcakes, Delicious Food for Diabetes,
Easter, Fresh Baked, Good Fast Family Food, Good Food
for Mums, Kids' Baking, The Lemon and Lime Cookbook,
M&S Chocolate, The Natural Menopause Cookbook,
Olive + Oil, The Pumpkin Cookbook, Vanilla, Veggie Food
for Kids, Viva Italia!*

Contents

Introduction

Many people find the prospect of baking a cake rather daunting. They are perfectly happy to try their hand at the most complicated dinner party recipes and are perhaps confident enough to whip up a delicious meal from whatever happens to be in the refrigerator. However, when it comes to whisking, weighing, lining and timing, they admit defeat before they've even begun. This book is here to dispel all those baking myths and to show you that there is nothing complicated or difficult about making mouthwatering cakes, pastries and biscuits.

The rise of the cake

The hectic pace of modern living has resulted in a dramatic increase in all things quick and easy. Ready meals, prepared salads, frozen foods and precooked meat and vegetables have all been introduced to help save time and take the pressure out of cooking and eating. However, only a generation or two ago, most people cooked all their meals from scratch, and this would also include baking their own cakes and biscuits.

Many people learned an appreciation of food and cooking as they helped their parents or grandparents in the kitchen, delighting in the permitted mess and waiting patiently for freshly baked muffins or fairy cakes to cool enough to eat. Despite the ready-made alternatives that are available today, these memories survive, and many people still find

the time to do their own baking. In fact, there's something of a baking renaissance, thanks in part to the increase in popularity of farmers' markets and artisan bakeries. Once you're used to the wonderful aroma and taste of a freshly baked muffin or cookie, it's hard to go back to something in a plastic wrapper. This has encouraged novice cooks to try their hand at making their own cakes, and they have found that after a little practice it's easy to incorporate baking into a busy schedule.

You are what you eat

With so many articles about what we eat in the media, people are becoming increasingly aware of their diets and the ingredients that go into their meals. As with any dish you prepare yourself, when you make a cake or batch of muffins you know exactly what's in them, and the list of ingredients is bound to be a lot shorter and more straightforward than anything you will find in a shop. This means that you can use your favourite brand of flour or butter or even use organic products, if you prefer. Food allergies can also be more easily catered for if you do your own baking.

Homemade cakes and biscuits are more cost-effective compared with shop-bought varieties. Many of the recipes for biscuits and small cakes make large batches, and the price per biscuit will often be just a few pence. There's also a great sense of achievement when you take a perfectly risen cake out of the oven or when you serve homemade scones or cookies to guests. If you get really confident, why not give cakes to people for presents? A birthday cake with a personalized message on top or some delicious Florentines (see page 94) in a pretty box tied with ribbon would make a lovely gift.

You will find ideas for every possible occasion in this book. Each recipe has clear instructions, so you'll feel confident whether you are a novice cook or already have some experience of baking. Many recipes are perfect for families to prepare together, so set aside a Saturday afternoon and get your children involved.

Baking terms, tips and techniques

Below, you will find information and tips for the main areas of baking, as well as explanations of some important terms.

Biscuits

There is an infinite variety of biscuits, and you'll find a whole chapter dedicated to biscuits and cookies in this book. They're made in a similar way to cakes and use the same techniques – ingredients are melted in, whisked or creamed together. However, as biscuits are usually thin and quite delicate, the dough is treated differently. You shouldn't spoon biscuit or cookie dough on to a hot baking sheet, because this will cause the base to burn. You should also allow reasonable space between the biscuits, because the dough will spread out when it begins to heat in the oven. Always have an extra baking sheet ready for use, just in case it's needed.

Cakes

A basic cake recipe consists of flour, sugar, fat (butter, margarine or oil) and eggs. Popular flavourings include chocolate, citrus, coffee, nuts, spices and dried fruit, but your options are virtually limitless. You'll find a diverse selection of cake recipes to choose from here including easy, classic cakes, such as Upside-down Pineapple Sponge (see page 59) and Malty Fruit Cake (see page 69), to more elaborate creations for special occasions, such as the luxurious Easter Nest Torte (see page 121).

There are a few important points to remember when you are making cakes.

• Make sure that bowls are scrupulously clean when you whisk egg whites; the smallest speck of dust or grease can ruin the eggs.

• Try not to open the oven door while the cake is cooking, particularly at the beginning. The batter is at a delicate stage and needs a constant heat in order to rise.

• If you are not sure if your cake is cooked through properly, insert a metal skewer into the centre of the cake, hold it there briefly

patience to perfect it. However, if you want to make your own sweet flans, pies and pastries then it's a good idea to learn how to make pastry. You can buy ready-made puff pastry and you might want to use this for the first couple of recipes or keep some in the kitchen in case of emergencies!

Shortcrust pastry

This popular pastry is used extensively in both sweet and savoury dishes. It's basically made with half the amount of fat to flour, with egg sometimes added to produce a rich shortcrust pastry.

then remove. If the skewer is dry and clean, the cake is cooked; if it is not, you need to return the cake to the oven and test it again a few minutes later.

• When you remove a cake from the oven, give it a few minutes to begin cooling in the tin. This means the cake will start to contract and will be easier to remove. Once the cake is cool enough to handle you can transfer it to a wire rack to cool completely.

Creaming

This technique is used in many cake recipes. It involves beating together the sugar and fat with a wooden spoon or electric mixer. The butter should be at room temperature before you begin so that it is pliable and easy to work. Beat the butter with the sugar until you have a light, aerated mixture. You then mix in the eggs and flour, usually adding a spoon of each alternately because the eggs need to be added gradually.

Choux pastry

Famously used to make profiteroles (see page 113), this is actually a batter that's piped from a bag rather than being rolled out. The batter makes buns, which are baked in the oven and then filled with cream.

Rubbing in

This technique is used more in denser cakes and biscuits. You don't need utensils for this one – it's time to get your hands messy! Put the flour in a mixing bowl, then add the butter in small pieces. You then simply take small amounts of the mixture at a time and literally rub it between your fingers and thumbs until it resembles breadcrumbs. At this point you can stir in the additional ingredients and bring the mixture together to form a dough.

Puff pastry

This incredibly light, delicate pastry is made of thin layers of dough that are separated by butter. It rises to create a large volume but it melts in the mouth. Pastry making is an art, and it does require a lot of practice and

Melting chocolate

When recipes require the addition of melted chocolate, break or chop it into pieces and put it into a small, heatproof bowl set above simmering water. Take care that the base of the bowl does not touch the water and make sure that no droplets of water get into the chocolate when you remove the bowl from the saucepan. Stir the melting chocolate once or twice, but do not overstir or it will lose its glossiness. Buy the best-quality cooking chocolate you can find – those containing more than 70 per cent cocoa solids have the best flavour and texture.

Storecupboard ingredients

You'll find that a relatively small number of essential ingredients will be sufficient to prepare a vast array of cakes. Obviously, cakes for special occasions and some unusual recipes will require a trip to the shops, but if you keep a good stock of the following you can get baking simple cakes immediately.

Butter

In recent years many people have started to put margarine instead of butter on their toast. However, when it comes to baking there's no substitute for the real thing. The rich, creamy taste of butter makes it ideal for most biscuit and cake recipes. Buy an unsalted variety and, unless otherwise specified, take it out of the refrigerator in good time before you begin cooking so that it is soft and easy to work.

Oil

A few recipes call for oil instead of butter and this will usually be sunflower oil. Occasionally you may need olive oil – don't interchange them though, as each has a unique taste.

Flour

You will mainly use self-raising or plain flour in sweet baking recipes. Plain flour is made from wheat, although there are many variations that are produced from other grains and cereals. Self-raising flour is produced in the same way but, as its name suggests, it already has a raising agent (baking powder) in it, as well as a small amount of salt. If you need self-raising flour for a recipe but don't have any at home, you can easily make your own by simply adding 1 teaspoon baking powder to each 250 g (8 oz) of plain flour. Both plain and self-raising flours are available in white and wholemeal varieties. It's a good idea to stock up on both if you plan to do a lot of baking.

Eggs

Another essential baking ingredient, eggs act as a binding substance for the dry ingredients and also help cakes and pastries to rise. The great thing about homemade baking is that you can choose to use free-range and organic eggs, which can be more flavoursome and have rich, deep-orange yolks. Eggs should be at room temperature when you're using them for baking, so take them out of the refrigerator about half an hour before you need them.

Raising agents

The raising agent is what makes your cake rise when it's in the oven. There are many different types of raising agent, but the two most commonly used are baking powder and bicarbonate of soda. They work by reacting with an acidic ingredient, heat, water or other elements to produce carbon dioxide. This makes bubbles, which then increase the volume of the batter. Be careful to use exactly the amount required for a recipe.

Yeast
Yeast is most commonly used in bread, but you will also find it in some sweet baking recipes. It adds both flavour and texture to a recipe, but its main purpose is to add bulk. Dough expands with the addition of yeast and becomes lighter and more aerated.

Sugar
Cakes and biscuits wouldn't taste the same without the addition of sugar! It obviously sweetens the cake but, as sugar melts at high temperatures, it will also add some moisture. You will probably use caster sugar for most of your baking, which is finer than granulated sugar so it blends more smoothly with other ingredients. However, you might also need granulated, icing sugar and raw cane sugar on occasions. Check the recipe before you begin.

Essential equipment
Although you can make cakes with the equipment in any moderately well-stocked kitchen, if you are going to do a lot of baking you will find it useful to have the items described below. You will also find it useful to have a pastry brush, spatula, oven gloves, a rolling pin and a palette knife.

Food processor and electric mixer
If you intend to make a lot of cakes both a food processor and an electric mixer will be invaluable additions to your kitchen. Of course, you can mix everything by hand but this is a more laborious process.

Electric hand whisk
This is a great little gadget for whisking smaller quantities of ingredients or beating cream.

Kitchen scales
Many baking recipes rely for their success on the accuracy of the measurements. Even a slight variation in the quantity of sugar or flour added will have an impact on the finished cake. For a really accurate reading, opt for electric scales.

Paper, knives, scissors
You will need greaseproof paper and nonstick baking paper for a number of recipes. A good set of knives is an essential addition to the kitchen and you will need a large and small knife for chopping. Scissors will come in

handy when a recipe requires you to cut paper to fit cake tins and also for cutting pastry shapes.

Tins, sheets and racks

You will need cake tins (decide on which size will work best for you) and muffin tins – deep for muffins and regular for smaller cakes, such as fairy cakes. Two or three baking sheets should be sufficient, and you will also need a wire rack for turning out and cooling cakes.

Spoons

A set of measuring spoons will prove invaluable, while wooden spoons are necessary for mixing ingredients, especially for creaming butter and sugar.

Measuring bowls and jugs

You should have a selection of mixing bowls in different sizes, because you will often have to use more than one in a recipe, including a heatproof bowl for melting chocolate. They stack away inside each other so they won't take up too much room in your kitchen. Measuring jugs are needed for liquids.

Sieves

You may need more than one sieve, and it's a good idea to have a regular sieve and one with a finer mesh for more delicate ingredients, such as icing sugar, or for when ingredients need to be finely sieved together.

Storage

Storage is an important part of baking. Although it's not uncommon for freshly baked cakes and biscuits to disappear before they're cool enough to transfer to the biscuit tin, you might want to try and save a couple at least! Many people do their baking in one or two big sessions every few weeks and, if this is the case, there may be a number of different items to store away. It would be a real shame to lose a carefully prepared cake because of dampness in the container.

The best container for a cake is a metal tin because there's no risk of damp, as there can be with plastic. You should wrap the cake in two layers of greaseproof paper or some kitchen foil before placing it in the cake tin to stop the cake from drying out. Cookies and biscuits should be stored in an airtight container and, as with cakes, they should be kept somewhere cool and dry. Don't keep them in the refrigerator, where they can develop mould.

Freezing

Most cakes can be frozen successfully. You should always use an appropriate freezer-proof container and make sure it's rigid if your cake has decorations. Alternatively, wrap the cake in freezer foil. Some people like to slice the cake into individual portion sizes before freezing. This means you don't have to defrost the whole cake if you only need a couple of slices at a time.

Biscuits can also be frozen, and you can either keep them on a flat tin wrapped in foil or store them in a rigid freezer-proof container. If you're making cookies, you can freeze any leftover dough or make a double batch and freeze half for a later date. Make sure any cakes, bakes or biscuits are completely cool before you freeze them.

Small cakes and bakes

The ideal accompaniment for morning coffee or afternoon tea, dainty little sponge cakes, freshly made scones or slices of tasty gingerbread are easy to make and require little time in the oven. Use different coloured icing to decorate fairy cakes or melt good-quality chocolate to give an extra-delicious topping for a special treat.

Strawberry choux puffs

makes **12 cakes**
preparation time **40 minutes,**
   plus infusing
cooking time **35 minutes**

50 g (2 oz) plain flour
50 g (2 oz) unsalted butter,
   diced
2 eggs, beaten
1 teaspoon vanilla extract
500 g (1 lb) strawberries,
   thinly sliced
icing sugar, for dusting

CREME PATISSIERE
   (CONFECTIONERS' CUSTARD)
150 ml (¼ pint) milk
150 ml (¼ pint) double cream
1 vanilla pod
4 egg yolks
45 g (1½ oz) caster sugar
25 g (1 oz) plain flour

1 Make the crème pâtissière. Put the milk and cream in a heavy-based saucepan. Score the vanilla pod lengthwise, add it to the pan and bring the mixture to the boil. Remove the pan from the heat and leave to infuse for 20 minutes. Beat together the egg yolks, sugar and flour until smooth. Remove the vanilla pod from the milk, scrape out the seeds and return them to the milk. Pour the milk over the egg mixture, beating well.

2 Return the custard to the pan and cook over a gentle heat, stirring constantly with a wooden spoon, for 4–5 minutes until it is thick and smooth. Turn the custard into a small bowl, cover with a circle of greaseproof paper or clingfilm to prevent a skin from forming and leave to cool.

3 Make the pastry. Sift the flour on to a sheet of greaseproof paper. Melt the butter in a saucepan with 150 ml (¼ pint) water. Bring the mixture to the boil, then remove the pan from the heat. Tip in the flour and beat until the mixture forms a ball that comes away from the sides of the pan. Cool for 2 minutes, then gradually beat in the eggs until the mixture is smooth and glossy. Add the vanilla extract.

4 Lightly grease a large baking sheet and sprinkle with water. Put 12 even-size spoonfuls of the mixture, spaced well apart, on the sheet and bake in a preheated oven, 200°C (400°F), Gas Mark 6, for about 25 minutes or until they are well risen and golden. Make a slit around the middle of each and return to the oven for 3 minutes to dry out. Transfer to a wire rack to cool. Open out each puff and divide the strawberries among them. Pile the crème pâtissière on top and push the puffs back together so the strawberries and crème pâtissière still show around the centre. Dust with icing sugar and store in a cool place until you are ready to serve.

Chocolate fairy cakes with butter icing

makes **12 cakes**
preparation time **20 minutes**
cooking time **about 20 minutes**

**175 g (6 oz) unsalted butter,
softened
125 g (4 oz) caster sugar
125 g (4 oz) self-raising flour
3 eggs
125 g (4 oz) ground almonds or
hazelnuts
50 g (2 oz) unblanched
hazelnuts, coarsely
chopped and toasted
75 g (3 oz) white chocolate,
chopped
75 g (3 oz) milk chocolate,
chopped**

**ICING
250 g (8 oz) unsalted butter,
softened
50 g (2 oz) Vanilla Sugar
(see page 43)
125 g (4 oz) icing sugar
2 teaspoons lemon juice**

1 Put the butter, sugar, flour, eggs and ground almonds or hazelnuts in a bowl and beat the mixture for 1–2 minutes until pale and creamy.

2 Reserve a handful of the chopped unblanched hazelnuts for decoration and add the remainder to the creamed mixture with the white and milk chocolates. Mix together.

3 Line a 12-section muffin tin with paper cases and spoon the cake mixture into the cases. Bake the cakes in a preheated oven, 180°C (350°F), Gas Mark 4, for about 20 minutes or until they are risen and just firm to the touch. Transfer to a wire rack to cool.

4 Make the icing. Beat together the butter, sugars and lemon juice in a bowl until pale and fluffy. Spread the icing over the cakes with a small spatula and decorate with the reserved nuts.

Orange and lemon fairy cakes

makes **12 cakes**
preparation time **20 minutes**
cooking time **15–20 minutes**

2 eggs
125 g (4 oz) caster sugar
50 g (2 oz) unsalted butter
125 g (4 oz) self-raising flour
1 tablespoon finely grated
lemon rind
2 tablespoons orange flower
water
2–3 tablespoons milk

TO DECORATE
325 g (11 oz) icing sugar,
sifted
1½ tablespoons orange juice
1½ tablespoons lemon juice
yellow and orange food
colouring
finely pared orange and
lemon rind coated in
caster sugar

1 Put the eggs, sugar, butter, flour and lemon rind in a large bowl and beat until smooth. Add the orange flower water and enough milk to give the mixture a good dropping consistency.

2 Line a 10-section deep muffin tin with paper cases. Spoon the mixture into the cases and cook in a preheated oven, 200°C (400°F), Gas Mark 6, for 15–20 minutes or until risen and golden. Remove from the oven and transfer to a wire rack to cool.

3 Slice the tops off the cakes. Mix half the icing sugar with the orange juice in one bowl and the other half with the lemon juice in another. Dot a tiny amount of the relevant food colouring into each and stir until you have 2 pastel-coloured icings.

4 Use a teaspoon to pour a small amount of the orange icing over 6 of the cakes so that it covers the surface evenly. Repeat with the yellow icing over the remaining cakes. Decorate the cakes with orange and lemon rind, pressing the rind on lightly before leaving the icing to set completely.

Easter cakes

makes **12 cakes**
preparation time **20 minutes,**
 plus setting
cooking time **15–18 minutes**

125 g (4 oz) plain flour
175 g (6 oz) caster sugar
175 g (6 oz) unsalted butter,
 softened
1½ teaspoons baking powder
1½ teaspoons vanilla extract
2 eggs

TOPPING
175 g (6 oz) icing sugar, sifted
½ teaspoon vanilla extract
3–4 teaspoons water
a few drops of yellow, green
 and pink food colouring
selection of jelly beans,
 to decorate

1 Put all the cake ingredients in a bowl and beat with a wooden spoon or electric mixer until smooth.

2 Line a 12-section muffin tin with paper cases, spoon the mixture into the cases and bake in a preheated oven, 180°C (350°F), Gas Mark 4, for 15–18 minutes or until well risen and the cakes spring back when pressed gently with a fingertip. Leave to cool in the tin.

3 Make the topping. Mix together the icing sugar, vanilla extract and enough water to make a smooth icing. Divide the icing into 3 bowls and colour each batch. Take the cakes from the tin, ice them and decorate with jelly beans. Leave for 30 minutes for the icing to set before serving.

Mocha fairy cakes

makes **12 cakes**
preparation time **15 minutes,**
    plus cooling
cooking time **20 minutes**

250 ml (8 fl oz) water
250 g (8 oz) caster sugar
125 g (4 oz) unsalted butter,
    diced
2 tablespoons cocoa
    powder, sifted
½ teaspoon bicarbonate
    of soda
2 tablespoons coffee granules
225 g (7½ oz) self-raising flour
2 eggs, lightly beaten

TOPPING
150 g (5 oz) plain dark
    chocolate, chopped
150 g (5 oz) unsalted butter,
    diced
2 tablespoons golden syrup
12 chocolate-covered coffee
    beans, to decorate

1 Put the measurement water and sugar in a saucepan and heat gently, stirring, until the sugar has dissolved. Stir in the butter, cocoa powder, bicarbonate of soda and coffee granules and bring to the boil. Simmer for 5 minutes, remove from the heat and set aside to cool.

2 Beat the flour and eggs into the cooled chocolate mixture until smooth. Line a 12-section muffin tin with paper cases and spoon the mixture into the cases. Bake in a preheated oven, 180°C (350°F), Gas Mark 4, for 20 minutes or until risen and firm. Cool on a wire rack.

3 Make the icing. Put the chocolate, butter and syrup in a bowl set over a pan of gently simmering water until melted, stirring occasionally. Remove from the heat and leave to cool to room temperature, then chill until thickened. Spread over the cakes, top each with a chocolate-covered coffee bean and leave to set.

Frosted primrose cakes

makes **12 cakes**
preparation time **30 minutes,**
  plus setting
cooking time **18–20 minutes**

VANILLA FAIRY CAKES
150 g (5 oz) unsalted butter,
  softened
150 g (5 oz) caster sugar
175 g (6 oz) self-raising flour
3 eggs
1 teaspoon vanilla extract

WHITE CHOCOLATE
  FUDGE ICING
200 g (7 oz) white chocolate,
  chopped
5 tablespoons milk
175 g (6 oz) icing sugar

TO DECORATE
selection of small spring
  flowers, such as primroses,
  violets or rose petals
1 egg white, lightly beaten
caster sugar, for dusting
narrow pastel-coloured
  ribbon, to decorate

1 Make the cakes. Put all the ingredients in a mixing bowl and whisk for 1–2 minutes until light and creamy. Line a 12-section muffin tin with paper cases and spoon the mixture into the cases. Bake in a preheated oven, 180°C (350°F), Gas Mark 4, for 18–20 minutes or until risen and just firm to the touch. Transfer to a wire rack to cool.

2 Make the chocolate fudge icing. Put the chocolate and milk in a heatproof bowl, set over a saucepan of gently simmering water, and leave until melted, stirring occasionally. Remove the bowl from the pan and stir in the icing sugar until smooth.

3 Make sure the flowers are clean and thoroughly dry before you ice the cakes. Put the egg white in a small bowl and the sugar in another. Use your fingers or a soft brush to coat all the petals on both sides with egg white. Dust plenty of sugar over the flowers until evenly coated. Transfer to a sheet of nonstick baking paper and leave for at least 1 hour until firm.

4 Use a small palette knife to spread the chocolate icing over the tops of the cakes while they are still warm. Decorate the top of each with the frosted flowers, tie a length of ribbon around each paper case and finish in a bow.

Strawberry cream cakes

makes **12 cakes**
preparation time **30 minutes**
cooking time **18–20 minutes**

**12 Vanilla Fairy Cakes
   (see page 21)**
**300 g (10 oz) small
   strawberries**
150 ml (¼ pint) double cream
2 teaspoons caster sugar
½ teaspoon vanilla extract
4 tablespoons redcurrant jelly
1 tablespoon water

1 Use a small, sharp knife to scoop out the centre of each cake to leave a deep cavity. Reserve 6 of the smallest strawberries and thinly slice the remainder.

2 Whip the cream with the sugar and vanilla extract until just peaking. Spoon a little into the centre of each cake and flatten slightly with the back of the spoon.

3 Arrange the sliced strawberries, overlapping, around the edges of each cake. Halve the reserved strawberries and place a strawberry half in the centre of each cake.

4 Heat the redcurrant jelly in a small, heavy-based saucepan with the measurement water until melted, then brush over the strawberries. Store the cakes in a cool place until ready to serve.

Hot cross buns

makes **12 buns**
preparation time **1 hour,**
 plus proving
cooking time **20 minutes**

**375 g (12 oz) strong bread
 flour**
150 ml (¼ pint) lukewarm milk
**4 tablespoons lukewarm
 water**
**25 g (1 oz) fresh yeast or
 2 tablespoons active
 dry yeast**
1 teaspoon caster sugar
1 teaspoon salt
½ teaspoon mixed spice
½ teaspoon ground cinnamon
½ teaspoon grated nutmeg
50 g (2 oz) caster sugar
**50 g (2 oz) unsalted butter,
 melted**
1 egg, beaten
175 g (6 oz) currants
**75 g (3 oz) mixed peel,
 chopped**
**50 g (2 oz) shortcrust pastry
 (thawed if frozen)**
butter, to serve

GLAZE
3 tablespoons caster sugar
**4 tablespoons milk and
 water mixed**

1 Put about 50 g (2 oz) flour in a small bowl. Add the milk and water and blend in the yeast and 1 teaspoon sugar. Mix this into the flour and leave in a warm place for about 15 minutes for fresh yeast and 20 minutes for dry. Meanwhile, sift the remaining flour, salt, spices and sugar into a large bowl.

2 Allow the butter to cool but not to harden. Add it to the frothy yeast mixture with the beaten egg. Stir this into the flour and mix well with a wooden spoon. Scatter the currants and mixed peel into the mixture and mix to a fairly soft dough. Add a spoonful of water if necessary.

3 Turn out the dough on to a lightly floured surface and knead well. Put it into an oiled polythene bag and allow to rise for 1–1½ hours at room temperature until doubled in size. Turn on to a floured surface and knock back.

4 Divide the dough into 12 and shape the pieces into small buns. Press down briefly on each bun with the palm of your hand and place the buns, spaced well apart, on a floured baking sheet. Cover and put in a warm place for 20–30 minutes or until doubled in size.

5 Meanwhile, roll out the pastry thinly and cut 24 narrow strips about 8 cm (3 inches) long. When the buns have risen, dampen the pastry strips and lay 2 across each bun to make a cross. Bake the buns in a preheated oven, 190°C (375°F), Gas Mark 4, for 20 minutes or until they are golden-brown and firm to the touch.

6 Make the glaze by dissolving the sugar in the milk and water mixture over a low heat. When the buns are ready, brush them twice with the glaze, then serve them hot, split and buttered.

Mini raspberry sandwich cakes

makes **12 cakes**
preparation time **15 minutes**
cooking time **10–12 minutes**

**175 g (6 oz) unsalted butter,
softened**
175 g (6 oz) caster sugar
175 g (6 oz) self-raising flour
3 eggs
**4 tablespoons seedless
raspberry jam**
fresh raspberries, to decorate
**2 tablespoons caster sugar or
sifted icing sugar**

1 Put the butter, sugar, flour and eggs in a bowl and beat together until smooth.

2 Line a 12-section deep muffin tin with circles of greaseproof paper and brush the paper lightly with oil. Spoon the cake mixture into the tin and smooth with the back of the teaspoon.

3 Bake in a preheated oven, 180°C (350°F), Gas Mark 4, for 10–12 minutes or until the cakes are well risen and golden and the tops spring back when pressed with a fingertip. Loosen the sides of the cakes with a round-bladed knife then transfer to a wire rack to cool.

4 Cut each cake in half then spread the lower halves with the jam. Replace the cake tops, add the raspberries and sprinkle with a little icing sugar.

Chocolate-orange brownies

makes **16 brownies**
preparation time **15–20**
 minutes
cooking time **30 minutes**

250 g (8 oz) orange-flavoured
 dark chocolate or plain dark
 chocolate with 1 teaspoon
 orange essence
250 g (8 oz) unsalted butter
175 g (6 oz) caster sugar
4 eggs, lightly beaten
finely grated rind of 1 orange
175 g (6 oz) plain flour
pinch of salt
1 teaspoon baking powder
150 g (5 oz) milk chocolate,
 roughly chopped
75 g (3 oz) macadamia nuts,
 roughly chopped

1 Put the dark chocolate and butter in a heavy-based saucepan over a low heat until just melted. Remove from the heat, stir in the sugar and set aside to cool a little. Pour the melted chocolate into a large bowl and beat in the eggs, orange rind and orange essence (if used).

2 Sift the flour, salt and baking powder into the bowl and fold in, together with the chocolate pieces and macadamia nuts. Grease and line a cake tin, about 20 x 30 x 5 cm (8 x 12 x 2 inches), and pour the mixture into the tin.

3 Cook in a preheated oven, 180°C (350°F), Gas Mark 4, for 25–30 minutes or until the cake mixture is set but not too firm. Leave to cool in the tin, then cut into squares and serve.

Cranberry, oatmeal and cinnamon scones

makes **10 scones**
preparation time **10 minutes**
cooking time **12 minutes**

175 g (6 oz) self-raising flour
1 teaspoon baking powder
1 teaspoon ground cinnamon
75 g (3 oz) unsalted butter,
    diced
75 g (3 oz) caster sugar
50 g (2 oz) oatmeal, plus extra
    for sprinkling
75 g (3 oz) dried cranberries
5–6 tablespoons milk
beaten egg or milk, to glaze
butter, to serve

1 Put the flour, baking powder and cinnamon in a bowl, add the butter and rub it in with your fingertips until the mixture resembles breadcrumbs. Add the sugar and oatmeal and mix to combine.

2 Add the cranberries and milk and mix together until the mixture forms a soft dough, adding a little more milk if necessary to achieve this consistency.

3 Turn out on to a lightly floured surface and roll out to 1.5 cm (¾ inch) thick. Cut out rounds with a 5 cm (2 inch) cutter and transfer them to a lightly greased baking sheet. Reroll the trimmings to make more scones.

4 Brush the tops with beaten egg or milk and sprinkle with oatmeal. Bake in a preheated oven, 220°C (425°F), Gas Mark 7, for 10–12 minutes or until risen and golden. Transfer to a wire rack to cool. Serve split and buttered.

Apricot and white chocolate rockies

makes **24 biscuits**
preparation time **15 minutes**
cooking time **12–15 minutes**

250 g (8 oz) self-raising flour
125 g (4 oz) unsalted butter,
  diced
75 g (3 oz) caster sugar
100 g (3½ oz) ready-to-eat
  dried apricots, cut into
  small pieces
100 g (3½ oz) white chocolate,
  chopped
1 egg
2–3 tablespoons milk

1 Sift the flour into a bowl, add the butter and rub it in with your fingertips until the mixture resembles breadcrumbs. Stir in the sugar, apricots and chocolate, add the egg then mix in enough milk to make a soft, lumpy-looking mixture.

2 Use a dessertspoon and teaspoon to scoop and drop 24 mounds of the mixture on to lightly oiled baking sheets, leaving a little space between each. Bake in a preheated oven, 180°C (350°F), Gas Mark 4, for 12–15 minutes or until the biscuits are pale golden and just firm to the touch. Loosen with a palette knife and transfer to a wire rack to cool.

Sweet orange flower and honey baklava

makes **about 20 pieces**
preparation time **40 minutes,
plus cooling**
cooking time **1 hour**

**250 g (8 oz) blanched
almonds**
**150 g (5 oz) blanched
hazelnuts**
75 g (3 oz) caster sugar
150 g (5 oz) unsalted butter
**50 ml (2 fl oz) extra virgin
olive oil**
**300 g (10 oz) filo pastry
(22 sheets), trimmed
slightly to fit the tin**

SYRUP
300 g (10 oz) caster sugar
250 ml (8 fl oz) water
**50 ml (2 fl oz) extra virgin
olive oil**
**50 ml (2 fl oz) orange flower
water**
finely pared rind of 1 lemon
**3 tablespoons clear Greek
honey**
1 cinnamon stick

1 Make the syrup. Combine all the ingredients in a small saucepan and heat gently, stirring occasionally, until the sugar has dissolved. Increase the heat slightly and leave to bubble gently, without stirring, for about 20 minutes until it forms a light, sticky syrup. Remove the pan from the heat and allow the syrup to cool in the pan. Cover the pan and chill in the refrigerator, without straining.

2 Put the almonds, hazelnuts and sugar in a food processor and pulse until the nuts are chopped but not ground.

3 Melt the butter with the olive oil in a small, heavy-based saucepan over a low heat, then brush generously over a piece of filo pastry, keeping the remaining pastry covered with a damp tea towel. Butter a 20 x 30 x 5 cm (8 x 12 x 2½ inch) tin and line it with the sheet of pastry. Trim the pastry to fit the tin, leaving a little extra to allow for the pastry to shrink during cooking. Repeat the process using 4 more sheets of pastry, brushing them with the butter and oil mixture as you layer them.

4 Scatter the pastry with one-third of the nuts and cover them with 5 more sheets of pastry, brushing them with the butter and oil mixture as you go. Add half the remaining nuts and then cover them with 5 more sheets of pastry, the remaining nuts and then the remaining 7 sheets of pastry. Brush the top liberally with the remaining butter and oil mixture. Use a sharp knife to cut through the top few layers of pastry in a crisscross pattern to make about 20 diamond shapes. Bake in a preheated oven, 190°C (375°F), Gas Mark 5, for about 40 minutes until golden.

5 Remove the cinnamon and lemon rind from the syrup. As soon as you take the baklava from the oven, pour the syrup evenly over it. Leave to cool, then cut into scored diamonds.

Raspberry and coconut friands

makes **9 cakes**
preparation time **10 minutes**
cooking time **18–20 minutes**

75 g (3 oz) **plain flour**
200 g (7 oz) **icing sugar**
125 g (4 oz) **ground almonds**
50 g (2 oz) **desiccated coconut**
grated rind of 1 lemon
5 egg whites
175 g (6 oz) **unsalted butter,**
melted
125 g (4 oz) **raspberries**
icing sugar, for dusting

1 Sift the flour and icing sugar into a bowl and stir in the ground almonds, coconut and lemon rind.

2 Whisk the egg whites in a separate bowl until they are frothy and fold them into the dry ingredients. Add the melted butter and stir until evenly combined.

3 Spoon the mixture into 9 lightly oiled friand tins (or a muffin tin). Top each friand with a few raspberries and bake in a preheated oven, 200°C (400°F), Gas Mark 6, for 18–20 minutes or until a skewer inserted into the centre of one of the friands comes out clean. Leave to cool for 5 minutes in the tins and then turn out on to a wire rack to cool completely. Dust with icing sugar and store in a cool place until ready to serve.

Millionaire's shortbread

makes **18 squares**
preparation time **15 minutes,
plus chilling**
cooking time **20–25 minutes**

250 g (8 oz) plain flour
25 g (1 oz) cornflour
50 g (2 oz) caster sugar
**175 g (6 oz) unsalted butter,
diced**

TOPPING
2 tablespoons golden syrup
75 g (3 oz) unsalted butter
**75 g (3 oz) light muscovado
sugar**
3 tablespoons double cream
**75 g (3 oz) plain dark or milk
chocolate**
75 g (3 oz) white chocolate

1 Put the flour, cornflour and sugar in a large bowl, add the butter and rub it in with your fingertips until the mixture resembles breadcrumbs. Squeeze the crumbs together then tip the mixture into a lightly oiled, 30 x 20 cm (12 x 8 inch) tin and press it flat. Bake in a preheated oven, 180°C (350°F), Gas Mark 4, for 20–25 minutes or until it is pale golden.

2 When the shortbread is almost ready put the golden syrup, butter and sugar in a saucepan and heat until the butter has melted. Boil for 1 minute. Stir in the cream and cook for 30 seconds. Pour the hot toffee over the hot shortbread, smooth flat, then leave to cool and set.

3 Break the plain or milk chocolate into pieces, place in a heatproof bowl set over just boiled water and leave for 4–5 minutes until melted. Drizzle spoonfuls of the melted chocolate in lines over the set toffee. Chill for 15 minutes. Melt the white chocolate and drizzle over the top. Chill until set. Cut the shortbread into 18 pieces and remove from the tin.

Danish pastries

makes **12 pastries**
preparation time **45 minutes**
cooking time **30–40 minutes**

**2 x 375 g (12 oz) blocks
bought puff pastry (thawed
if frozen) or double
quantity homemade puff
pastry (see page 124)**
**½ quantity crème pâtissière
(see page 14)**
3 apricots, halved and pitted
25 g (1 oz) flaked almonds
**6 tablespoons light soft
brown sugar**
**2 large plums, peeled, pitted
and diced**

EGG GLAZE
1 egg
2 tablespoons milk

APRICOT GLAZE
125 g (4 oz) apricot jam
1 teaspoon lemon juice
1 teaspoon water

1 Roll out the pastry thinly on a lightly floured surface and cut it into 12 squares, each 12 x 12 cm (5 x 5 inches). Place these squares on 2 large, lightly oiled baking sheets. Make the egg glaze by whisking together the egg and milk with a hand-held whisk.

2 Put a heaped tablespoon of crème pâtissière in the middle of 6 squares and spread it over the pastry, leaving a 1 cm (½ inch) border. Arrange 6 apricot halves over the crème pâtissière, brush the edges with egg glaze and scatter over some flaked almonds and soft brown sugar. Bake in a preheated oven, 200°C (400°F), Gas Mark 6, for 15–20 minutes or until risen and golden.

3 Meanwhile, make the apricot glaze. Put the jam in a small saucepan with the lemon juice and water and heat gently until the jam melts. Increase the heat and boil for 1 minute. Remove from the heat and press through a fine sieve. Remove the cooked pastries from the oven, transfer to a wire rack and brush all over with warm apricot glaze.

4 Place a heaped tablespoon of crème pâtissière in the middle of the remaining 6 squares and top with the diced plums. Cut a diagonal slit from each corner of the dough to meet the filling, then take alternate points of the dough and turn them up and over to meet in the centre of the crème pâtissière, pressing them together gently to form a windmill shape. Brush the exposed edges of the pastry with egg glaze and scatter with almonds and sugar. Bake for 15–20 minutes or until risen and golden. Brush with warm apricot glaze and leave to cool on a wire rack.

Lamingtons

makes **24 cakes**
preparation time **20 minutes,
    plus standing**
cooking time **25–30 minutes**

**125 g (4 oz) unsalted butter,
    softened
125 g (4 oz) caster sugar
2 eggs, lightly beaten
250 g (8 oz) self-raising flour,
    sifted
pinch of salt
4 tablespoons milk
1 teaspoon vanilla extract**

ICING
**400 g (13 oz) icing sugar
100 g (3½ oz) cocoa powder
150–175 ml (5–6 fl oz) boiling
    water
200 g (7 oz) desiccated
    coconut**

1 Put the butter and sugar in a bowl and beat together until pale and fluffy. Beat in the eggs, a little at a time, until incorporated. Sift in the flour and salt and fold into the creamed mixture with the milk and vanilla extract.

2 Oil and base-line a 18 x 25 cm (7 x 10 inch) cake tin and transfer the mixture to the tin. Smooth the surface with a palette knife and bake in a preheated oven, 190°C (375°F), Gas Mark 5, for 25–30 minutes or until risen and firm to the touch. Leave to cool in the tin for 5 minutes and then turn out on to a wire rack to cool. Leave out overnight.

3 Make the icing. Sift the icing sugar and cocoa powder into a bowl, make a well in the centre and beat in the boiling water to make a smooth icing with a pouring consistency.

4 Cut the cooled cake into 24 squares. Use 2 forks to dip each cake into the icing and then immediately coat with coconut. Leave to set on nonstick baking paper.

Muffins

Muffins are sweet, cup-shaped cakes, best made in paper cases, which can have almost any flavour you wish. They can be left plain, topped with a simple sprinkling of sugar or decorated with icing or a creamy topping. Whatever the predominant flavour, however, all muffins are best eaten on the day they are made.

Carrot and orange muffins

Makes **6 muffins**
Preparation time **15 minutes**
Cooking time **15–20 minutes**

150 g (5 oz) self-raising flour
½ teaspoon baking powder
75 g (3 oz) caster sugar
finely grated rind and juice of
** 1 orange**
125 g (4 oz) carrots, coarsely
** grated**
100 ml (3½ fl oz) soya milk
2 eggs, beaten
2 tablespoons sunflower oil
1 tablespoon apricot jam,
** warmed**

1 Sift the flour and baking powder into a bowl and add the sugar, orange rind and grated carrot. Mix together and make a well in the centre. In a separate bowl mix together the milk, eggs, orange juice and oil. Pour the liquid into the flour and stir until just blended.

2 Line 6 sections of a muffin tin with paper cases and fill the cases two-thirds full with the mixture. Cook in a preheated oven, 200°C (400°F), Gas Mark 6, for 15–20 minutes or until a skewer inserted into the centre of a muffin comes out clean. Transfer the muffins to a wire rack to cool.

3 Brush the tops of the muffins with a little warmed apricot jam and serve immediately.

White chocolate and orange muffins

Makes **12 muffins**
Preparation time **10 minutes**
Cooking time **20–25 minutes**

125 g (4 oz) plain flour
2 teaspoons baking powder
125 g (4 oz) caster sugar
generous pinch of salt
3 tablespoons sunflower oil
1 large egg
150 ml (¼ pint) milk
finely grated rind of 1 orange
150 ml (¼ pint) orange juice
1 teaspoon orange essence
150 g (5 oz) white chocolate,
 chopped

1 Sift together the flour and baking powder and stir in the sugar and salt. In a separate bowl beat together all the remaining ingredients, except the chocolate, until blended. Pour the egg and milk mixture into the dry ingredients, add the chocolate and stir briefly until barely combined. The mixture should still be lumpy.

2 Line a 12-section muffin tin with paper cases and spoon the mixture into the cases. Cook in a preheated oven, 200°C (400°F), Gas Mark 6, for 20–25 minutes or until the muffins are risen and golden.

3 Leave to cool for a few minutes in the pan, then transfer the muffins, still in the paper cases, to a wire rack until they are cool enough to eat.

Cranberry, orange and vanilla muffins

Makes **12 muffins**
Preparation time **10 minutes**
Cooking time **15–20 minutes**

75 g (3 oz) unsalted butter,
   melted
175 ml (6 fl oz) milk
1 egg
finely grated rind of 1 orange
1 teaspoon vanilla extract
300 g (10 oz) self-raising flour
2 teaspoons baking powder
125 g (4 oz) dried cranberries
50 g (2 oz) soft brown sugar

VANILLA SUGAR
½ vanilla pod
50 g (2 oz) caster sugar

1 Make the vanilla sugar in advance. Use a small, sharp knife to cut the ½ vanilla pod in half lengthways to make 2 pieces. Put the sugar in a glass jar and push the vanilla pieces into it. Cover with a lid and store for about a week before using, shaking the jar occasionally to disperse the vanilla flavour.

2 Mix together the butter, milk, egg, orange rind and vanilla extract. Sift the flour and baking powder into a bowl and stir in the cranberries, the light brown sugar and 50 g (2 oz) vanilla sugar. Add the milk mixture to the bowl and stir briefly until only just combined.

3 Line a 12-section muffin tin with paper cases, spoon the mixture into the cases, piling it up in the centre, and bake in a preheated oven, 190°C (375°F), Gas Mark 5, for 15–20 minutes or until they are well risen and golden-brown. Transfer to a wire rack to cool slightly and serve warm.

Prune and vanilla muffins

Makes **12 muffins**
Preparation time **15 minutes**
Cooking time **18–20 minutes**

50 g (2 oz) sugar lumps
300 g (10 oz) plain flour
3 teaspoons baking powder
125 g (4 oz) light muscovado
sugar
175 g (6 oz) ready-to-eat,
dried, pitted prunes,
roughly chopped
3 eggs, lightly beaten
4 tablespoons sunflower oil
50 g (2 oz) unsalted butter,
melted
1½ teaspoons vanilla extract
150 ml (¼ pint) natural yogurt

1 Put the sugar lumps into a plastic bag and roughly crush them with a rolling pin.

2 Put the flour, baking powder and muscovado sugar into a large bowl, add the prunes and stir to mix. Beat together the eggs, oil, butter and vanilla extract in a small bowl and add to the flour mixture. Add the yogurt and stir gently until just combined.

3 Line a 12-section deep muffin tin with paper cases and spoon the mixture into the cases. Sprinkle with the crushed sugar and bake in a preheated oven, 190°C (375°F), Gas Mark 5, for 18–20 minutes or until well risen and the tops have cracked. Serve while still warm.

Cranberry muffins

Makes **15 muffins**
Preparation time **10 minutes**
Cooking time **20 minutes**

1 egg
100 ml (3½ fl oz) milk
75 g (3 oz) unsalted butter,
** softened**
150 g (5 oz) plain flour, sifted
3 teaspoons baking powder
100 g (3½ oz) caster sugar
75 g (3 oz) frozen cranberries,
** partially defrosted**

TOPPING
2 tablespoons caster or
** icing sugar**
1 teaspoon cinnamon

1 Put the egg and milk in a bowl, whisk together and beat in the softened butter.

2 Sift together the flour and baking powder and stir into the mixture with the sugar. Mix thoroughly until smooth, then add the cranberries, folding them in gently.

3 Grease and flour a 15-section muffin tin (or use 2 tins) and spoon the mixture into the tin until each is three-quarters full.

4 Mix together the ingredients for the topping and sprinkle over the muffins. Bake in a preheated oven, 180°C (350°F), Gas Mark 4, for 20 minutes or until firm to the touch. Let the muffins cool in the tins for 2–3 minutes, then turn them out and serve immediately.

Blackcurrant and almond muffins

Makes **12 muffins**
Preparation time **10 minutes**
Cooking time **20–25 minutes**

200 g (7 oz) plain flour
2 teaspoons baking powder
½ teaspoon bicarbonate
  of soda
pinch of salt
50 g (2 oz) caster sugar
few drops of almond essence
75 g (3 oz) unsalted butter,
  melted
200 ml (7 fl oz) buttermilk
300 g (10 oz) can blackcurrants
  in natural juice, drained, or
  250 g (8 oz) fresh or frozen
  blackcurrants
40 g (1½ oz) flaked almonds

1 Sift together the flour, baking powder, bicarbonate of soda and salt into a bowl, then stir in the sugar.

2 Mix together the almond essence, melted butter, buttermilk and blackcurrants in a separate bowl, then lightly stir in the dry ingredients. The mixture should still look a little lumpy.

3 Line a 12-section deep muffin tin with paper cases. Spoon the mixture into the cases, sprinkle over the flaked almonds and bake in a preheated oven, 190°C (375°F), Gas Mark 5, for 20–25 minutes or until risen and golden. Carefully lift the cases from the tin and transfer them to a wire rack to cool. These muffins are best eaten on the day they are made.

Pumpkin and raisin muffins

Makes **12 muffins**
Preparation time **15 minutes**
Cooking time **50 minutes**

**500 g (1 lb) pumpkin, peeled,
deseeded and cut into
chunks**
250 g (8 oz) plain flour
2 teaspoons baking powder
**¼ teaspoon bicarbonate
of soda**
100 g (4 oz) soft brown sugar
½ teaspoon salt
¼ teaspoon ground cinnamon
¼ teaspoon ground nutmeg
50 g (2 oz) raisins
2 eggs, lightly beaten
125 ml (4 fl oz) milk
**50 g (2 oz) unsalted butter,
melted**

1 Steam or boil the pumpkin chunks for 15–20 minutes until tender and drain thoroughly. Purée in a blender or food processor and strain. Set aside.

2 Sift together the flour, baking powder, bicarbonate of soda, sugar, salt, cinnamon and nutmeg into a large bowl. Stir in the raisins and set aside.

3 Put the pumpkin purée in a separate bowl and beat in the eggs, milk and butter. Fold into the flour mixture until the dough is just combined.

4 Lightly butter a 12-section deep muffin tin and spoon the mixture into the tins, filling each one about two-thirds full. (If necessary, make 2 batches.) Bake in a preheated oven, 200°C (400°F), Gas Mark 6, for 25–30 minutes or until a skewer inserted into the centre of a muffin comes out clean. Leave in the tin for 1–2 minutes and then transfer to a wire rack to cool completely.

Pumpkin, courgette and Parmesan muffins

Makes **12 muffins**
Preparation time **15 minutes**
Cooking time **50 minutes**

500 g (1 lb) pumpkin, peeled,
   deseeded and cut into
   chunks
250 g (8 oz) plain flour
1 teaspoon baking powder
½ teaspoon bicarbonate
   of soda
1 teaspoon salt
¼ teaspoon nutmeg
125 g (4 oz) courgette, grated
1 large egg, lightly beaten
125 ml (4 fl oz) milk
50 g (2 oz) unsalted butter,
   melted
50 g (2 oz) finely grated fresh
   Parmesan cheese

1 Steam or boil the pumpkin chunks for 15–20 minutes until tender and drain thoroughly. Purée in a blender or food processor and strain. Set aside.

2 Sift the flour, baking powder, bicarbonate of soda, salt and nutmeg together into a large bowl. Stir in the courgette.

3 Put the pumpkin purée in a separate bowl and beat in the egg, milk, butter and two-thirds of the Parmesan. Fold into the flour mixture until the batter is just combined.

4 Lightly butter a 12-section muffin tin and spoon the batter into the tin, sprinkling each with some of the remaining Parmesan. (If necessary, make 2 batches.) Bake in a preheated oven, 200°C (400°F), Gas Mark 6, for 25–30 minutes or until a skewer inserted into the centre of a muffin comes out clean. Leave in the tin for 1–2 minutes and then transfer to a wire rack to cool completely.

Cheesy corn muffins

Makes **12 muffins**
Preparation time **15 minutes**
Cooking time **15 minutes**

**125 g (4 oz) quick-cook
    polenta**
175 g (6 oz) self-raising flour
2 teaspoons baking powder
**100 g (3½ oz) mature Cheddar
    cheese, grated**
150 ml (¼ pint) milk
2 eggs, lightly beaten
2 teaspoons Dijon mustard
4 tablespoons sunflower oil
salt and pepper
butter, to serve

1 Put the polenta, flour and baking powder in a bowl and stir in the cheese. Beat together the milk, eggs, mustard and oil, add a little salt and pepper and add to the polenta mixture. Stir until just mixed.

2 Line a 12-section muffin tin with paper cases and spoon the mixture into the cases. Bake in a preheated oven, 200°C (400°F), Gas Mark 6, for 15 minutes or until the muffins are well risen and golden-brown. Loosen the edges of the paper cases with a round-bladed knife then transfer to a wire rack. Serve the muffins warm, broken and spread with butter. They are best eaten on the day they are made.

Big savoury muffins

Makes **12 muffins**
Preparation time **5 minutes**
Cooking time **20–25 minutes**

250 g (8 oz) self-raising flour
1 teaspoon baking powder
½ teaspoon bicarbonate
   of soda
pinch of salt
2 bacon rashers, grilled
   and chopped
3 spring onions, sliced
8 olives, pitted and roughly
   chopped
1 tablespoon chopped
   parsley
50 g (2 oz) Cheddar cheese,
   grated
6 tablespoons olive oil
125 ml (4 fl oz) semi-skimmed
   milk
pepper
butter, to serve

1 Sift together the flour, baking powder, bicarbonate of soda and salt into a large bowl. Add the bacon, spring onions, olives, parsley and cheese and stir together. Season to taste with pepper.

2 Mix together the oil and milk and lightly stir into the flour mixture to give a slightly lumpy mixture.

3 Line a 12-section muffin tin with paper cases and spoon the mixture into the cases. Bake in a preheated oven, 190°C (375°F), Gas Mark 5, for 20–25 minutes until golden and risen. Carefully lift the cases from the tin and transfer to a wire rack to cool.

4 Serve split in half and spread with some butter. These muffins are best eaten on the day they are made.

Quick and easy bakes

Mouthwatering cakes don't take all day to make. You need only spend a quarter of an hour mixing and blending fresh ingredients, and then you can get on with other things while your cakes and bakes are cooking, filling your home with delicious aromas. E-numbers and preservatives will be things of the past, while you give your family cakes and bakes that contain only the finest, best-quality ingredients.

Blueberry and vanilla loaf

Serves **8**
Preparation time **15 minutes**
Cooking time **40–45 minutes**

**125 g (4 oz) unsalted butter,
  softened**
125 g (4 oz) caster sugar
2 eggs
150 g (5 oz) self-raising flour
½ teaspoon baking powder
125 g (4 oz) ground almonds
2 teaspoons vanilla extract
150 g (5 oz) blueberries
**Vanilla Sugar (see page 43),
  for dusting**

1 Put the butter, sugar, eggs, flour, baking powder, ground almonds and vanilla extract in a bowl and beat until pale and creamy. Fold in two-thirds of the blueberries.

2 Grease and line the base and sides of a 500 g (1 lb) loaf tin with a double thickness of greaseproof paper, making sure that the paper comes 2.5 cm (1 inch) above the rim. Turn the mixture into the prepared pan, level the top and sprinkle with the remaining blueberries.

3 Bake in a preheated oven, 180°C (350°F), Gas Mark 4, for 40–45 minutes or until the cake is well risen and firm to the touch. Leave to cool in the tin for 10 minutes.

4 Turn out the cake on to a wire rack and sprinkle the top generously with vanilla sugar. Transfer to a serving plate.

Sugared angel cake

Serves **12**
Preparation time **20 minutes**
Cooking time **30–35 minutes**

8 egg whites
1 teaspoon cream of tartar
1½ teaspoons vanilla bean
  paste
1 teaspoon finely grated
  lemon rind
250 g (8 oz) caster sugar
175 g (6 oz) plain flour, plus
  extra for dusting
Vanilla Sugar (see page 43), for
  dusting
fresh raspberries, to decorate
whipped cream, to serve

1 Beat the egg whites in a large, clean bowl until they are frothy. Add the cream of tartar and beat again until the egg whites are softly peaking. Beat in the vanilla bean paste and the lemon rind.

2 Gradually beat in the caster sugar, a tablespoon at a time, beating well between each addition, until the mixture is glossy. Sift the flour over the mixture and gently fold it in with a large metal spoon.

3 Lightly grease and flour a 23 cm (9 inch) springform ring mould. Turn the mixture into the prepared tin, level the surface and bake in a preheated oven, 160°C (325°F), Gas Mark 4, for 30–35 minutes or until it is firm to the touch and a skewer inserted into the centre comes out clean.

4 Invert the tin on to a wire rack and leave the cake to cool upside down. When the cake is completely cold, loosen the edges with a knife and turn it on to a serving plate.

5 Generously dust the cake with vanilla sugar and surround with raspberries to decorate. Serve with whipped cream.

Upside-down pineapple sponge

Serves **6**
Preparation time **5 minutes**
Cooking time **1 hour**

**100 g (3½ oz) unsalted butter,
  softened**
**100 g (3½ oz) self-raising flour,
  sifted**
50 g (2 oz) caster sugar
2 eggs
few drops vanilla extract
1 tablespoon golden syrup
**4 canned pineapple slices in
  juice, drained**
**ready-made custard or
  natural yogurt, to serve**

1 Put the butter, flour, sugar, eggs and vanilla extract in a bowl and beat together until smooth.

2 Lightly grease and flour a 600 ml (1 pint) pudding basin and spoon in the syrup. Place the pineapple slices around the base of the basin, then pour in the sponge mixture.

3 Cover the basin with foil, then put in a saucepan. Add boiling water so that it comes halfway up the sides of the basin and steam for 1 hour, topping up with more boiling water as necessary.

4 Carefully lift the basin from the saucepan, remove the foil and turn the pudding out on to a serving plate. Serve with custard or yogurt.

Victoria sandwich

Serves **8**
Preparation time **5 minutes**
Cooking time **25–30 minutes**

**250 g (8 oz) unsalted butter,
    softened**
**250 g (8 oz) caster sugar, plus
    extra for serving**
4 eggs, lightly beaten
250 g (8 oz) self-raising flour
pinch of salt
1 tablespoon milk
1 teaspoon vanilla extract
**raspberry or strawberry jam,
    for filling**

1 Cream together the butter and sugar in a bowl until pale and fluffy. Gradually beat in the eggs, a little at a time, adding a little of the flour if the mixture starts to curdle. Beat in the salt, milk and vanilla extract, then sift the remaining flour into the bowl and fold it in using a large metal spoon.

2 Grease and base-line 2 round cake tins, each 20 cm (8 inch) across. Divide the mixture equally between the tins and bake in a preheated oven, 180°C (350°F), Gas Mark 4, for 25–30 minutes or until risen and firm to the touch. Remove from the oven, leave to cool in the tins for 5 minutes and then transfer the cakes to a wire rack to cool.

3 Sandwich the sponges together with jam and serve dusted with caster sugar.

wierd texture!!

Lemon drizzle cake

Serves **8**
Preparation time **20 minutes,**
  plus standing
Cooking time **20–25 minutes**

5 eggs
125 g (4 oz) caster sugar
pinch of salt
125 g (4 oz) plain flour
1 teaspoon baking powder
finely grated rind of 1 lemon
1 tablespoon lemon juice
100 g (3½ oz) unsalted butter,
  melted and cooled
crème fraîche or soured
  cream, to serve

SYRUP
225 g (7½ oz) icing sugar
125 ml (4 fl oz) lemon juice
finely grated rind of 1 lemon
seeds scraped from 1
  vanilla pod

1 Put the eggs, sugar and salt in a large heatproof bowl set over a pan of barely simmering water. Beat the mixture for 2–3 minutes or until it triples in volume and thickens to the consistency of lightly whipped cream. Remove from the heat.

2 Sift in the flour and baking powder, add the lemon rind and juice and drizzle the butter down the sides of the bowl. Fold in gently with a large metal spoon.

3 Grease and line a 23 cm (9 inch) square cake tin (do not use a loose-based tin). Spoon the mixture into the tin and bake in a preheated oven, 180°C (350°F), Gas Mark 4, for 20–25 minutes or until it is risen, golden and coming away from the sides of the tin.

4 Meanwhile, put all the ingredients for the syrup into a small saucepan and heat gently until the sugar has dissolved. Increase the heat and boil rapidly for 4–5 minutes or until you have a light syrup. Set aside to cool a little.

5 Remove the cake from the oven and leave to stand for 5 minutes. Make holes all over the surface with a skewer and drizzle over two-thirds of the warm syrup. Leave the cake to cool and absorb the syrup in the tin.

6 Carefully remove the cake from the tin and peel away the lining paper. Place it on a dish and serve in squares or slices with a spoonful of crème fraîche or soured cream and an extra drizzle of syrup.

Apple and plum cake with almonds

Serves **12**
Preparation time **10 minutes**
Cooking time **1 hour**

250 g (8 oz) plain flour
2 teaspoons baking powder
175 g (6 oz) caster sugar
3 eggs
grated rind of 1 orange
100 g (3½ oz) unsalted butter,
    melted
2 tablespoons semi-skimmed
    milk
2 dessert apples, peeled,
    cored and chopped
8 plums, pitted and chopped
25 g (1 oz) flaked almonds
Greek yogurt, to serve
    (optional)

1 Sift together the flour and baking powder into a bowl. In a separate bowl whisk together the sugar and eggs until pale and thick.

2 Gently fold the flour mixture, orange rind, butter and milk into the egg mixture.

3 Lightly grease and line a 23 cm (9 inch) round cake tin and pour the mixture into the tin. Scatter the fruit and flaked almonds over the top of the cake (much of the fruit will sink into the mixture) and bake in a preheated oven, 180°C (350°F), Gas Mark 4, for 1 hour until firm to touch. Leave to cool a little in the tin, then transfer to a wire rack.

4 Serve warm or cold. If you want to turn this cake into a special dessert, serve with some Greek yogurt. The cake may be stored for up to 2 days in an airtight container.

Carrot and lime cake

Serves **8–10**
Preparation time **20 minutes,**
plus cooling
Cooking time **about 1 hour**

250 g (8 oz) lime marmalade
2 tablespoons freshly
squeezed lime juice
150 g (5 oz) carrots, finely
grated
175 g (6 oz) raisins
125 g (4 oz) unsalted butter,
softened
125 g (4 oz) light brown sugar
2 eggs
250 g (8 oz) self-raising
wholewheat flour

TOPPING
175 g (6 oz) cream cheese
2 teaspoons clear honey
1 tablespoon lime juice
1 tablespoon shredded
lime rind

1 Heat the marmalade and lime juice together in a small saucepan until the marmalade has melted. Remove the pan from the heat and stir in the carrots and raisins. Leave to cool.

2 Put the butter and sugar in a large bowl and beat together until light and fluffy. Add the eggs, one at a time, beating well after each addition, until the mixture is thick and smooth.

3 Pour the cooled carrot mixture into the bowl and add the flour, carefully folding it in with a large metal spoon until evenly blended.

4 Lightly grease and base-line a 23 cm (9 inch) springform cake tin. Spoon the mixture into the tin, level the top and bake in a preheated oven, 160°C (325°F), Gas Mark 3, for about 1 hour or until the cake springs back when the centre is lightly pressed.

5 Loosen the edge of the cake with a palette knife and release the tin. Remove the base, peel away the paper and leave the cake to cool on a wire rack.

6 Make the topping. Beat the cream cheese, honey and lime juice in a bowl. Spread the topping evenly over the top of the cake and decorate with lime rind.

Pineapple, vanilla and anise drizzle cake

Serves **8–10**
Preparation time **20 minutes,
  plus infusing**
Cooking time **1¼ hours**

5 whole star anise
6 tablespoons lemon juice
**250 g (8 oz) unsalted butter,
  softened**
300 g (10 oz) caster sugar
2 teaspoons vanilla extract
4 eggs, beaten
300 g (10 oz) self-raising flour
**250 g (8 oz) sweetened dried
  pineapple, coarsely chopped**
**50 g (2 oz) Vanilla Sugar
  (see page 43)**

1 Put the star anise, lemon juice and 3 tablespoons water in a small saucepan, cover and heat gently for 3 minutes. Remove from the heat and leave to infuse.

2 Meanwhile, beat together the butter, 250 g (8 oz) caster sugar and the vanilla extract until pale and fluffy. Gradually beat in the eggs, a little at a time, adding a little of the flour if the mixture starts to curdle. Sift the remaining flour into the bowl and fold it in using a large metal spoon. Stir in two-thirds of the pineapple.

3 Lightly grease and base-line an 18 cm (7 inch) square or a 20 cm (8 inch) round cake tin. Turn the mixture into the tin, level the top and sprinkle with the remaining pineapple. Bake in a preheated oven, 160°C (325°F), Gas Mark 3, for about 1¼ hours or until it is risen and firm to the touch.

4 Add the vanilla sugar and the remaining caster sugar to the lemon and anise in the pan and drizzle the syrup over the cake while it is still warm.

Marbled apricot and banana cake

Serves **8**
Preparation time **20 minutes,
plus cooling**
Cooking time **about 30 minutes**

**250 g (8 oz) ready-to-eat dried
apricots**
**200 ml (7 fl oz) apple juice
or water**
**175 g (6 oz) unsalted butter,
softened**
100 g (3½ oz) caster sugar
**2 small ripe bananas, 250 g
(8 oz) unpeeled weight,
mashed**
200 g (7 oz) self-raising flour
1 teaspoon baking powder
3 eggs, beaten
icing sugar, for dusting

FILLING
200 g (7 oz) cream cheese
2 tablespoons icing sugar
**grated rind and juice of
½ orange**

1 Put the apricots in a saucepan with the apple juice or water, cover and simmer gently for 10 minutes. Cool slightly, then purée the fruit with the juice in a food processor or blender until smooth. Set aside to cool.

2 Put the butter and sugar in a bowl and beat together until light and fluffy. Beat the bananas into the creamed mixture.

3 Sift the flour with the baking powder and gradually beat into the banana mixture alternately with the beaten eggs.

4 Lightly oil and base-line 2 round 20 cm (8 inch) sandwich tins. Divide the cake mixture evenly between the tins, dot the apricot purée over the surface, then swirl a knife through the two mixtures to marble them. Bake in a preheated oven, 180°C (350°F), Gas Mark 4, for about 20 minutes or until well risen and golden and the cakes spring back when pressed with a fingertip. Leave in the tin for 15 minutes, then turn out on to a wire rack, peel off the lining paper and leave to cool completely.

5 Make the filling. Beat together the cream cheese with the icing sugar, orange rind and juice and use to sandwich the cooled cakes together. Transfer the cake to a serving plate and dust with icing sugar.

Malty fruit cake

Makes **10 slices**
Preparation time **10 minutes**
Cooking time **about 45 minutes**

100 g (3½ oz) **bran cereal**
75 g (3 oz) **dark muscovado**
  sugar
150 g (5 oz) **raisins or sultanas**
350 ml (12 fl oz) **semi-**
  skimmed milk
2 pieces **preserved stem**
  ginger in syrup, drained
  and finely chopped
125 g (4 oz) **self-raising**
  wholemeal flour

1 Put the bran cereal, sugar, raisins or sultanas and milk in a bowl and mix together. Leave to stand for 10 minutes until the cereal has softened and the mixture is pulpy. Add the ginger and stir to mix.

2 Sift the flour over the ingredients, tipping in any grains left in the sieve. Fold the ingredients together.

3 Lightly grease and line the base and long sides of a 1 kg (2 lb) loaf tin. Turn the mixture into the tin and bake in a preheated oven, 180°C (350°F) Gas Mark 4, for about 45 minutes or until just firm. Leave to cool in the tin. When it is cool, remove the cake from the tin and store in an airtight container for up to 5 days. Serve cut into slices.

Moist banana and carrot cake

Serves **14**
Preparation time **10 minutes**
Cooking time **1 hour 40 minutes**

**175 g (6 oz) ready-to-eat dried
   apricots, roughly chopped**
125 ml (4 fl oz) water
1 egg, lightly beaten
2 tablespoons clear honey
**100 g (3½ oz) walnuts, roughly
   chopped**
**4 ripe bananas, about 500 g
   (1 lb) unpeeled weight,
   mashed**
**1 large carrot, about 125 g
   (4 oz), grated**
**225 g (7½ oz) self-raising flour,
   sifted**

TOPPING
150 g (5 oz) cream cheese
2 tablespoons lemon curd

1 Put the apricots in a small saucepan with the measurement water, bring to the boil and simmer for 10 minutes. Allow to cool slightly then transfer to a liquidizer or food processor and blend to make a thick purée.

2 Put the egg, honey, walnuts, bananas, carrot and flour in a large bowl, add the apricot purée and mix well to combine.

3 Grease and line a 1 kg (2 lb) loaf tin, spoon the mixture into the tin and bake in a preheated oven, 180°C (350°F), Gas Mark 4, for 1½ hours or until a skewer inserted into the centre comes out clean. Turn out on to a wire rack to cool.

4 Beat together the cream cheese and lemon curd and spread over the top of the loaf. The cake may be stored for 2–3 days in the refrigerator.

Carrot and poppy seed cake

Makes **10 slices**
Preparation time **15 minutes**
Cooking time **about 40 minutes**

**200 g (7 oz) self-raising
  wholemeal flour**
1 teaspoon baking powder
**1 teaspoon ground mixed
  spice**
**250 g (8 oz) carrots, finely
  grated**
2 tablespoons poppy seeds
4 tablespoons molasses
125 g (4 oz) sultanas
2 eggs, lightly beaten
5 tablespoons olive oil
6 tablespoons milk

TOPPING
**125 g (4 oz) quark or other
  curd cheese**
2–3 tablespoons icing sugar

1 Sift the flour, baking powder and spice into a bowl, tipping in the grains left in the sieve. Add the carrots, poppy seeds, molasses and sultanas and stir until combined.

2 In a separate bowl lightly beat together the eggs, oil and milk. Add to the carrot mixture and fold the ingredients together gently.

3 Grease and line a round 18 cm (7 inch) cake tin. Turn the mixture into the tin, level the surface and bake in a preheated oven, 160°C (325°F), Gas Mark 3, for about 40 minutes until it is just firm to the touch. Transfer to a wire rack to cool.

4 Mix together the quark and icing sugar to make a smooth topping and spread it evenly over the cooled cake. Serve cut into slices.

Almondy fruit cake

Makes **10–12 slices**
Preparation time **15 minutes**
Cooking time **30–35 minutes**

250 g (8 oz) ready-to-eat dried apricots, roughly chopped
225 ml (7½ fl oz) water
75 g (3 oz) unsalted butter, diced
150 g (5 oz) dried figs, roughly chopped
50 g (2 oz) sultanas
100 g (3½ oz) whole blanched almonds, roughly chopped
50 g (2 oz) dark muscovado sugar
1 tablespoon lemon juice
200 g (7 oz) self-raising wholemeal flour
2 teaspoons baking powder
1 teaspoon ground cinnamon

1 Set aside 50 g (2 oz) of the apricots. Put the rest into a large saucepan with the measurement water and bring to a simmer. Cover and cook gently for about 5 minutes until the apricots have plumped up. Leave to cool slightly, then tip into a food processor or blender and blend to make a thick purée. Measure and make up the purée to 350 ml (12 fl oz) with more water if necessary.

2 Return the purée to the pan and stir in the butter until melted. Remove the pan from the heat, add the figs, sultanas, reserved apricots, nuts, sugar and lemon juice. Sift the flour, baking powder and cinnamon over the mixture, tipping in the grains left in the sieve. Gently fold the ingredients together.

3 Grease and line a shallow, round 20 cm (8 inch) cake tin. Turn the mixture into the tin and bake in a preheated oven, 190°C (375°F), Gas Mark 5, for 25–30 minutes or until just firm. Leave to cool in the tin. Serve cut into slices.

Chocolate, courgette and nut cake

Serves **12**
Preparation time **10 minutes**
Cooking time **40 minutes**

250 g (8 oz) courgettes,
    coarsely grated
2 eggs
100 ml (3½ fl oz) vegetable oil
grated rind and juice of
    1 orange
125 g (4 oz) caster sugar
225 g (7½ oz) self-raising flour
2 tablespoons cocoa powder
½ teaspoon bicarbonate
    of soda
½ teaspoon baking powder
50 g (2 oz) ready-to-eat dried
    apricots, chopped

TOPPING
200 g (7 oz) cream cheese
2 tablespoons chocolate-
    hazelnut spread
1 tablespoon hazelnuts,
    toasted and chopped

1 Put the courgettes in a sieve and squeeze out any excess liquid by pressing down on them.

2 Beat together the eggs, oil, orange rind and juice and sugar in a large bowl. Sift in the flour, cocoa powder, bicarbonate of soda and baking powder and beat to combine. Fold in the courgettes and apricots.

3 Grease and line a deep, loose-based, 20 cm (8 inch) cake tin. Spoon the mixture into the tin and bake in a preheated oven, 180°C (350°F), Gas Mark 4, for 40 minutes until risen and firm to the touch. Turn out on to a wire rack to cool.

4 Beat together the cream cheese and chocolate-hazelnut spread and spread the mixture over the top of the cake. Sprinkle over the hazelnuts. This cake may be stored for 2–3 days in an airtight container.

Whisked sponge with lemon curd

Serves **8**
Preparation time **15 minutes**
Cooking time **25–30 minutes**

6 eggs
175 g (6 oz) caster sugar
175 g (6 oz) plain flour, sifted
50 g (2 oz) unsalted butter,
melted
caster sugar, to dust

FILLING
150 ml (¼ pint) double cream
6 tablespoons lemon curd

1 Put the eggs and sugar in a bowl set over a pan of gently simmering water and whisk the eggs for 5 minutes until thickened to ribbon consistency.

2 Remove the bowl from the pan and gently fold in the flour and then the melted butter.

3 Lightly oil and base-line 2 round, 20 cm (8 inch) cake tins. Divide the mixture between the tins and bake in a preheated oven, 180°C (350°F), Gas Mark 4, for 25–30 minutes or until springy to the touch. Leave to cool in the tins for 5 minutes, then turn out on to a wire rack to cool completely.

4 Whip the cream until thick. Spread the lemon curd over one cake, top with the whipped cream and the second sponge. Dust with caster sugar and serve in wedges.

Gingerbread

Serves **24**
Preparation time **10 minutes**
Cooking time **1¼ hours**

500 g (1 lb) self-raising flour
1 tablespoon ground ginger
½ teaspoon bicarbonate
of soda
½ teaspoon salt
175 g (6 oz) soft brown sugar
175 g (6 oz) unsalted butter,
diced
175 ml (6 fl oz) black treacle
175 ml (6 fl oz) golden syrup
300 ml (½ pint) milk
1 egg, lightly beaten

1 Sift the flour, ground ginger, bicarbonate of soda and salt into a bowl. Put the sugar, butter, treacle and syrup into a saucepan and heat gently until the butter has melted and the sugar has dissolved.

2 Pour the treacle mixture into the dry ingredients together with the milk and egg and beat with a wooden spoon until the mixture is smooth.

3 Lightly oil and base-line a 20–30 cm (8–12 inch) baking tin. Spoon the mixture into the tin and bake in a preheated oven, 160°C (325°F), Gas Mark 3, for 1¼ hours or until a skewer inserted into the centre comes out clean. Leave to cool in the tin for 10 minutes and then turn out on to a wire rack to cool. Wrap the cooled cake in foil and store in an airtight container for up to 5 days.

Raspberry Swiss roll

Makes **8 slices**
Preparation time **20 minutes**
Cooking time **8–10 minutes**

4 eggs
125 g (4 oz) caster sugar, plus
extra for sprinkling
125 g (4 oz) plain flour
5 tablespoons raspberry jam
150 g (5 oz) fresh or frozen
raspberries, just thawed
pink and white sugar flowers,
to decorate

1 Put the eggs and sugar in a bowl set over a pan of simmering water. Beat together for 5 minutes until the mixture is thick enough to leave a trail when the whisk is lifted from the bowl. Remove from the heat and whisk until cool. Sift the flour over the top and gently fold it into the whisked mixture with a large metal spoon.

2 Lightly oil and line a 23 x 33 cm (9 x 13 inch) Swiss roll tin. Pour the mixture into the tin and smooth it gently into the corners. Bake in a preheated oven, 200°C (400°F), Gas Mark 6, for 8–10 minutes until the top is golden-brown and springs back when lightly pressed.

3 Put a damp tea towel on the work surface with a short edge towards you. Cover the tea towel with a piece of nonstick baking paper and sprinkle it with a little sugar.

4 Tip the cake and lining paper on to the baking paper. Remove the tin and peel away the lining paper. Spread the jam over the cake and sprinkle with two-thirds of the raspberries. Using the paper under the cake and the tea towel to help, roll up the cake from the edge nearest you, gradually peeling away the paper and cloth as you work. Wrap the paper tightly around the rolled cake and leave for 1–2 minutes. Transfer to a serving plate and decorate with the remaining raspberries and a few sugar flowers. Cut the cake into thick slices to serve.

Cherry streusel cake

Makes **16 squares**
Preparation time **15 minutes**
Cooking time **25–30 minutes**

175 g (6 oz) self-raising flour
100 g (3½ oz) unsalted butter,
    diced
75 g (3 oz) caster sugar
50 g (2 oz) ground almonds
1 egg, beaten
2 tablespoons milk
½ teaspoon almond essence
425 g (14 oz) can stoned black
    cherries, drained
25 g (1 oz) flaked almonds

1 Sift the flour into a bowl, add the butter and rub it in with your fingertips until the mixture resembles breadcrumbs. Add the sugar and ground almonds and stir with a wooden spoon to mix. Measure out 75 g (3 oz) of the crumb mixture and set it aside for the topping.

2 Add the egg, milk and almond essence to the rest of the mixture and mix together until smooth.

3 Lightly oil and line a shallow, square, 20 cm (8 inch) baking tin. Spoon the mixture into the tin and smooth flat. Spoon the cherries on top of the cake mixture and sprinkle over the reserved crumbs. Sprinkle the flaked almonds on top.

4 Bake in a preheated oven, 180°C (350°F), Gas Mark 4, for 25–30 minutes or until it is well risen and the topping is pale golden. Leave the cake to cool in the tin. Remove from the tin, peel away the paper and cut into 16 squares. The cake may be stored in an airtight tin for up to 2 days.

Moist and gooey chocolate cake

Serves **14–16**
Preparation time **30 minutes**
Cooking time **about 1 hour**

**400 g (13 oz) plain dark
  chocolate**
75 ml (3 fl oz) water
**175 g (6 oz) unsalted butter,
  softened**
**250 g (8 oz) light muscovado
  sugar**
4 eggs
100 g (3½ oz) self-raising flour
50 g (2 oz) cocoa powder
100 g (3½ oz) ground almonds
300 ml (½ pint) double cream
**250 g (8 oz) mascarpone
  cheese**

1 Gently melt 250 g (8 oz) of the chocolate with the measurement water in a small bowl. Beat together the butter and sugar until pale and creamy, then gradually beat in the eggs, adding a little of the flour if necessary to prevent the mixture from curdling. Stir in the chocolate.

2 Sift the remaining flour and cocoa powder over the bowl, add the almonds and fold gently into the cake mixture.

3 Lightly oil and line a round 20 cm (8 inch) cake tin. Turn the mixture into the tin, level the surface and bake in a preheated oven, 160°C (325°F), Gas Mark 3, for about 1 hour or until risen and just firm to the touch. The centre should still be slightly sticky if pierced with a skewer. Leave to cool in the tin.

4 Cut the cake into 3 horizontal layers. Lightly whip the cream and use it to sandwich the cake layers together on a serving plate.

5 Melt the remaining chocolate in a small bowl. Beat the mascarpone with 1 tablespoon boiling water. Beat in the melted chocolate and spread smoothly over the cake.

Coffee cake with pistachio praline

Serves **12**
Preparation time **40 minutes**
Cooking time **25–30 minutes**

6 eggs
175 g (6 oz) caster sugar
175 g (6 oz) plain flour, sifted
50 g (2 oz) unsalted butter, melted
2 tablespoons made espresso coffee, cooled

PRALINE
65 g (2½ oz) shelled pistachio nuts
125 g (4 oz) granulated sugar
50 ml (2 fl oz) water

MAPLE SYRUP ICING
6 egg yolks
175 g (6 oz) caster sugar
150 ml (¼ pint) milk
350 g (12 oz) unsalted butter (at room temperature), diced
3 tablespoons maple syrup

1 Put the eggs and sugar in a bowl set over a pan of gently simmering water. Whisk the eggs for 5 minutes until thickened. Remove the bowl from the heat and fold in the flour, melted butter and coffee.

2 Lightly grease and base-line a 23 cm (9 inch) cake tin. Spoon the mixture into the tin and bake in a preheated oven, 180°C (350°F), Gas Mark 4, for 25–30 minutes. Leave to cool in the tin for 5 minutes, then turn out on to a wire rack. Cut the cake into 3 horizontal layers.

3 Make the praline. Put the nuts on a baking sheet. Heat the sugar and water in a heavy-based saucepan until the sugar melts. Increase the heat and stir with a wooden spoon until the sugar turns light golden. Remove from the heat and pour over the nuts. Once set, break the praline into small pieces and then grind to a rough powder.

4 Make the icing. Beat together the egg yolks and sugar until pale and fluffy. Heat the milk until just boiling, then whisk into the egg mixture. Return to the pan and heat gently, stirring, until the mixture coats the back of the spoon. Remove the pan from the heat and beat the mixture for 2–3 minutes. Gradually beat in the butter, a little at a time, until the mixture is thick and glossy. Beat in the maple syrup.

5 Fold half the praline into half the icing and use it to sandwich the sponges together. Spread the remaining icing over the top and sides of the cake and sprinkle the reserved praline over the top.

Cookies and biscuits

Whether you are baking a classic recipe, such as shortbread or almond thins, or are trying an updated version of a traditional favourite like flapjacks, you can hardly go wrong with the easy instructions in this section. If there are any of these delicious biscuits and cookies left, remember to store them in an airtight container at room temperature.

Chocolate and vanilla cookies

Makes **18–20 cookies**
Preparation time **15 minutes**
Cooking time **15–20 minutes**

125 g (4 oz) unsalted butter,
softened
50 g (2 oz) caster sugar
50 g (2 oz) Vanilla Sugar
(see page 43)
1 egg
150 g (5 oz) porridge oats
150 g (5 oz) self-raising flour
250 g (8 oz) milk chocolate,
chopped

1 Put the butter and sugars in a bowl and beat together until pale and creamy. Beat in the egg, then add the oats and flour and stir until combined. Stir in the chocolate.

2 Place heaped dessertspoonfuls of the mixture on a lightly oiled baking sheet, spacing them well apart and flattening each one slightly with the back of a fork.

3 Bake in a preheated oven, 180°C (350°F), Gas Mark 4, for 15–20 minutes until the cookies are risen and pale golden. Leave on the baking sheet for 5 minutes to firm up slightly, then transfer to a wire rack to cool.

Peanut butter and banana cookies

Makes **about 28 cookies**
Preparation time **15 minutes**
Cooking time **10–15 minutes**

**125 g (4 oz) unsalted butter,
  softened**
150 g (5 oz) caster sugar
1 egg, beaten
1 teaspoon baking powder
**125 g (4 oz) crunchy peanut
  butter**
150 g (5 oz) plain white flour
**100 g (3½ oz) dried banana
  chunks, roughly chopped**
28 unsalted peanuts

1 Put all the ingredients, except the banana chunks and peanuts, in a blender or food processor and process until well mixed. Stir in the banana chunks. Roll the dough into balls about the size of a walnut and transfer them to lightly greased baking sheets, allowing enough space for the mixture to spread as it cooks. Flatten the balls slightly with the palm of your hand.

2 Press a whole peanut into the centre of each cookie and bake in a preheated oven, 190°C (375°F), Gas Mark 5, for 10–15 minutes or until the cookies are just beginning to brown around the edges.

3 Allow to cool slightly, then transfer to a wire rack to cool completely. Store in an airtight container for up to 5 days.

Vanilla fudge cookies

Makes **16 cookies**
Preparation time **15 minutes,**
 plus chilling
Cooking time **about 20 minutes**

200 g (7 oz) self-raising flour
1 teaspoon baking powder
125 g (4 oz) unsalted butter,
 diced
75 g (3 oz) soft brown sugar
1 egg
1 teaspoon vanilla extract
175 g (6 oz) vanilla fudge,
 finely chopped
Vanilla Sugar (see page 43),
 for dusting

1 Sift the flour and baking powder into a bowl, add the butter and rub it in with your fingertips until the mixture resembles breadcrumbs. Add the sugar and stir to mix.

2 Beat the egg with the vanilla extract and add to the bowl. Use your hands to mix it to a dough and turn it out on to a lightly floured surface. Shape the dough into a log about 20 cm (8 inches) long and wrap it in greaseproof paper. Chill for at least 1 hour.

3 Cut the log across into 16 thick slices and place them, spaced well apart, on a lightly greased baking sheet. Bake in a preheated oven, 180°C (350°F), Gas Mark 4, for about 15 minutes. Remove the cookies from the oven and sprinkle with the chopped fudge, pressing the pieces of fudge firmly into the dough. Return the cookies to the oven for a further 5 minutes or until they are turning golden. Take care that the fudge does not melt over the edges of the cookies.

4 Leave the cookies to stand on the baking sheet for 2 minutes, then transfer them to a wire rack. Leave to cool and serve dusted with vanilla sugar.

Easter cookies

Makes **18 cookies**
Preparation time **20 minutes,**
  plus setting
Cooking time **10 minutes**

250 g (8 oz) plain flour
25 g (1 oz) cornflour
175 g (6 oz) unsalted butter,
  diced
125 g (4 oz) caster sugar
a few drops of vanilla extract

TO DECORATE
½ sachet dried egg white or the
  equivalent of 1 egg white
375 g (12 oz) icing sugar, sifted
1 teaspoon lemon juice
selection of liquid or paste
  food colourings

1 Put the flour and cornflour in a bowl, add the butter and rub it in with your fingertips until the mixture resembles breadcrumbs. Add the sugar and vanilla extract and stir to mix. Bring the mixture together with your hands and squeeze it into a ball.

2 Knead lightly, then roll out thinly on a lightly floured surface. Stamp out appropriate shapes with biscuit cutters and transfer them to ungreased baking sheets. Reroll the trimmings and continue stamping until all the dough has been used.

3 Prick the cookies with a fork and bake in a preheated oven, 180°C (350°F), Gas Mark 4, for 10 minutes or until pale golden. Leave to cool on the baking sheet.

4 Make the icing. Mix the dried egg with water as indicated on the sachet. Gradually mix in the icing sugar and lemon juice to give a smooth consistency. Add extra water if the icing seems too thick. Divide in quarters and colour each portion to taste.

5 Spoon into paper piping bags, snip off the tips and ice the outlines around the edges of the cookie. Leave to dry. Then, fill in the rest of the surface of the cookie with the same colour icing to create a smooth, evenly covered surface. Leave to dry. Finally, pipe white icing over the top of the coloured surface to outline and make specific features.

Lemon butter cookies

Makes **about 50 cookies**
Preparation time **15 minutes,**
 plus chilling and cooling
Cooking time **10–12 minutes**

250 g (8 oz) unsalted butter
grated rind of 1 lemon
250 g (8 oz) granulated sugar
250 g (8 oz) flour, sifted

1 Put the butter and lemon rind in a bowl and beat together until creamy. Add the sugar and beat well. Stir in the flour. Cover and chill for 30 minutes.

2 Take teaspoonfuls of the mixture and roll lightly into balls. Place them on ungreased baking sheets and press down with a fork that has been dipped in cold water to prevent sticking. Bake in a preheated oven, 180°C (350°F), Gas Mark 4, for 10–12 minutes or until slightly browned.

3 Transfer the cookies to a wire rack to cool, then store in an airtight container.

Baby macaroons

Makes **about 24**
Preparation time **10 minutes**
Cooking time **20 minutes**

2 egg whites
125 g (4 oz) caster sugar
1 teaspoon vanilla bean paste
150 g (5 oz) ground almonds
125 g (4 oz) unsweetened
coconut
about 24 whole unblanched
almonds

1 Beat the egg whites until peaking, then gradually beat in the sugar, a tablespoon at a time, until the mixture is thick and glossy. Add the vanilla bean paste with the last of the sugar.

2 Gently fold in the ground almonds and coconut with a large metal spoon until evenly combined.

3 Use 2 teaspoons to place spoonfuls of the mixture, spaced slightly apart, on a lined baking sheet. Press a whole almond on the top of each macaroon and bake in a preheated oven, 180°C (350°F), Gas Mark 4, for 20 minutes or until they are pale golden and just firm to the touch. Leave to cool on the baking sheet.

Florentines

Makes **48 biscuits**
Preparation time **30 minutes**
Cooking time **about 10 minutes
per batch**

150 g (5 oz) **unsalted butter**
175 g (6 oz) **caster sugar**
4 tablespoons **double cream**
75 g (3 oz) **chopped mixed
peel**
50 g (2 oz) **glacé cherries,
chopped**
50 g (2 oz) **flaked almonds**
40 g (1½ oz) **dried cranberries**
25 g (1 oz) **pine nuts**
50 g (2 oz) **plain flour**
150 g (5 oz) **plain dark
chocolate**
150 g (5 oz) **white chocolate**

1 Put the butter and sugar in a saucepan and heat gently until the butter is melted. Increase the heat and bring the mixture to the boil. Immediately remove the saucepan from the heat, add the cream, mixed peel, cherries, almonds, cranberries, pine nuts and flour and stir well with a wooden spoon until evenly combined.

2 Lightly oil and line 2 large baking sheets. Drop 12 heaped teaspoonfuls of the mixture on to the sheets, leaving a 5 cm (2 inch) gap for the mixture to spread. Bake in a preheated oven, 180°C (350°F), Gas Mark 4, for 7 minutes. Remove from the oven and use an 8 cm (3 inch) biscuit cutter to drag the edges of the biscuits into neat rounds so that they are about 5 cm (2 inches) across. Bake for a further 3–4 minutes until golden around the edges. Remove from the oven and leave for 2 minutes. Carefully transfer the biscuits to baking paper and leave to cool. Repeat with the remaining mixture.

3 Melt the dark chocolate and white chocolate in separate bowls set over gently simmering water, stirring until the chocolate is smooth. Spoon the melted chocolate into separate paper icing bags and drizzle back and forth over the biscuits. Leave to set.

Almond thins

Makes **45–50 biscuits**
Preparation time **20 minutes**
Cooking time **40–45 minutes**

3 egg whites
100 g (3½ oz) caster sugar
½ teaspoon almond essence
100 g (3½ oz) plain flour
100 g (3½ oz) blanched
   almonds

1 Whisk the egg whites in a bowl until stiff and then whisk in the sugar and almond essence. Sift the flour over the egg whites and fold into the mixture until really smooth. Fold in the almonds.

2 Lightly oil and line a 1 kg (2 lb) loaf tin. Spoon the mixture into the tin and bake in a preheated oven, 180°C (350°F), Gas Mark 4, for 25 minutes or until the mixture is risen and golden. Remove from the oven, leave to cool for 5 minutes and then turn out on a wire rack to cool. Reduce the temperature to 140°C (275°F), Gas Mark 1.

3 Remove the paper and use a sharp knife to cut the block into wafer-thin slices. Put the slices on 2 large, oiled and lined baking sheets and bake for 15–20 minutes until lightly golden. Cool on a wire rack.

Mint chocolate sandwich

Makes **24–28 biscuits**
Preparation time **25 minutes,**
  plus chilling
Cooking time **10 minutes**

250 g (8 oz) plain flour
25 g (1 oz) cocoa powder
pinch of salt
200 g (7 oz) chilled unsalted
  butter, diced
100 g (3½ oz) icing sugar
2 egg yolks
1 teaspoon vanilla extract
250 g (8 oz) plain dark
  chocolate, chopped

FILLING
65 g (2½ oz) unsalted butter,
  softened
150 g (5 oz) icing sugar, sifted
1 teaspoon peppermint
  essence

1 Make the chocolate biscuit dough. Sift the flour, cocoa powder and salt into a bowl, add the butter and rub it in with your fingertips until the mixture resembles breadcrumbs. Add the sugar and mix, then add the egg yolks and vanilla extract. Beat until the mixture just starts to come together. Transfer the dough to a work surface and shape into a disc. Wrap in clingfilm and chill for 30 minutes.

2 Roll out the dough on a lightly floured surface until it is 3 mm (⅛ inch) thick. Use a 5 cm (2 inch) plain biscuit cutter to stamp out rounds. Put them on 3 large, oiled baking sheets and bake in a preheated oven, 200°C (400°F), Gas Mark 6, for 10 minutes or until they start to brown around the edges. Leave to cool on a wire rack.

3 Make the filling. Put the butter, icing sugar and peppermint essence in a bowl and beat together until smooth. Use it to sandwich the biscuits together.

4 Put the chocolate in a bowl set over a pan of gently simmering water and stir until melted. Put the biscuits, one at a time, on a fork and dip each one into the melted chocolate. Transfer to a sheet of baking paper to set and repeat with the remaining biscuits.

Classic shortbread

Makes **16 pieces**
Preparation time **15 minutes,
plus chilling**
Cooking time **18–20 minutes**

**250 g (8 oz) unsalted butter,
softened**
**125 g (4 oz) caster sugar, plus
extra for dusting**
250 g (8 oz) plain flour
125 g (4 oz) rice flour
pinch of salt

1 Put the butter and sugar in a bowl and cream together. Stir in the flour, rice flour and salt and work together to form a soft dough. Alternatively, put the butter and sugar in a food processor and process until pale and creamy. Sift in the remaining ingredients and process briefly until the ingredients just come together. Transfer to the work surface and knead gently to form a soft dough.

2 Shape the dough into a disc, wrap it in clingfilm and chill for 30 minutes.

3 Divide the dough in half and roll each piece out on a lightly floured surface to form 2 rounds, each 20 cm (8 inch) across. Transfer the rounds to 2 lightly oiled baking sheets. Score each piece with a sharp knife, marking it into 8 equal wedges, prick with a fork and flute the edges of the rounds with your fingers.

4 Sprinkle over a little caster sugar and bake in a preheated oven, 190°C (375°F), Gas Mark 5, for 18–20 minutes until golden. Remove from the oven and, while still hot, cut into wedges through the score marks. Leave to cool on the baking sheet for 5 minutes then transfer to a wire rack to cool. Store in an airtight tin.

Pistachio and pine nut biscotti

Makes **50 biscuits**
Preparation time **20 minutes**
Cooking time **50 minutes–1 hour**

175 g (6 oz) **shelled pistachio
   nuts**
2 tablespoons **pine nuts**
125 g (4 oz) **unsalted butter,
   softened**
200 g (7 oz) **granulated sugar**
2 **eggs, beaten**
finely grated **rind of 1 lemon**
1 tablespoon **Amaretto
   di Saronno**
375 g (12 oz) **plain white flour**
1½ teaspoons **baking powder**
½ teaspoon **salt**
75 g (3 oz) **coarse polenta**

1 Spread the pistachios and pine nuts on a baking sheet and toast in a preheated oven, 160°C (325°F), Gas Mark 3, for 5–10 minutes or until golden. Remove the nuts and leave to cool but leave the oven on.

2 Cream the butter with the sugar in a large bowl until just mixed. Beat in the eggs, lemon rind and Amaretto. Sift together the flour, baking powder and salt in a separate bowl, then stir into the butter mixture with the polenta. Stir in the pistachios and pine nuts.

3 Turn the dough on to a floured work surface and knead until smooth. The dough should be soft but not sticky.

4 Divide the dough into quarters. Roll each piece into a sausage 5 cm (2 inches) long and 1.5 cm (¾ inch) thick and flatten it slightly. Place the sausages on 2 lightly oiled baking sheets and bake in the preheated oven for about 35 minutes or until just golden around the edges.

5 Leave to cool slightly then cut diagonally into 1 cm (½ inch) thick slices. Place the biscotti, flat side down, on the baking sheets and bake for another 10–15 minutes or until golden-brown and crisp. Take care that they do not burn, or they will taste bitter. Transfer the biscotti to a wire rack to cool completely.

Apricot, fig and mixed-seed bites

Makes **24 biscuits**
Preparation time **10 minutes**
Cooking time **15 minutes**

150 g (5 oz) **unsalted butter**
75 g (3 oz) **soft light brown
sugar**
1 egg, beaten
2 tablespoons water
75 g (3 oz) **plain wholemeal
flour**
½ teaspoon bicarbonate
of soda
100 g (3½ oz) rolled oats
50 g (2 oz) ready-to-eat dried
apricots, chopped
50 g (2 oz) dried figs, chopped
50 g (2 oz) mixed seeds, such
as pumpkin, sunflower
and sesame

1 Put the butter and sugar in a bowl and cream together until light and fluffy. Beat in the egg and measurement water.

2 Sift together the flour and bicarbonate of soda, tipping any bran left in the sieve into the bowl. Add the oats, apricots, figs and seeds, then add to the egg mixture, stirring to combine.

3 Place walnut-sized pieces of the mixture on lined baking sheets and flatten them slightly with the back of a fork. Bake in a preheated oven, 180°C (350°F), Gas Mark 5, for 10–15 minutes or until golden, then cool on a wire rack. These bites will keep for 2 days in an airtight container.

Really fruity flapjacks

Makes **15–20 flapjacks**
Preparation time **15 minutes**
Cooking time **20 minutes**

100 g (3½ oz) unsalted butter
100 g (3½ oz) light muscovado
  sugar
5 tablespoons clear honey
375 g (12 oz) porridge oats
75 g (3 oz) ready-to-eat dried
  prunes, chopped
75 g (3 oz) ready-to-eat dried
  apricots, chopped
75 g (3 oz) raisins or sultanas
2 eggs, lightly beaten

1 Melt the butter with the sugar and honey in a saucepan. Remove from the heat and stir in the oats, prunes, apricots and raisins or sultanas until evenly mixed. Beat in the eggs.

2 Lightly grease a shallow 28–23 cm (11–9 inch) baking tin. Turn the mixture into the tin and level the surface. Bake in a preheated oven, 180°C (350°F), Gas Mark 4, for 20 minutes or until turning pale golden. Leave in the tin until almost cold, then cut into fingers and leave on a wire rack to cool completely. The flapjacks can be stored in an airtight container in a cool place for up to 5 days.

Cakes for special occasions

Nothing can equal the flavour and texture of a homemade cake, and when you are cooking for a special occasion it is worth taking the trouble to bake an especially rich or well-decorated cake. Make sure you have everything to hand before you begin, and you will find that the results will more than make up for the extra time and trouble you spend in making these luxuriously decadent cakes.

Chocolate and chestnut roulade

Serves **8**
Preparation time **20 minutes**
Cooking time **20 minutes**

**125 g (4 oz) plain dark
    chocolate, chopped**
5 eggs, separated
**175 g (6 oz) caster sugar, plus
    extra to sprinkle**
**2 tablespoons cocoa powder,
    sifted**
**250 g (8 oz) unsweetened
    chestnut purée**
4 tablespoons icing sugar
1 tablespoon brandy
250 ml (8 fl oz) double cream
icing sugar, to dust

1 Put the chocolate in a bowl set over a saucepan of gently simmering water until it has melted, stirring occasionally. Cool for 5 minutes.

2 Put the egg yolks in a separate bowl, add the sugar and whisk together for 5 minutes until pale and thickened. Stir in the melted chocolate and cocoa powder. Whisk the egg whites in a clean bowl until stiff and fold into the chocolate mixture until evenly combined.

3 Lightly oil and line a 23 x 33 cm (9 x 13 inch) Swiss roll tin. Transfer the mixture to the tin, spreading it well into the corners, and smooth the surface with a palette knife. Bake in a preheated oven, 180°C (350°F), Gas Mark 4, for 20 minutes or until risen and set.

4 Meanwhile, put a large sheet of nonstick baking paper on the work surface and sprinkle it with caster sugar. Remove the roulade from the oven and immediately turn it out on to the sugared paper. Carefully remove the tin and lining paper and cover the roulade with a clean tea towel. Set aside to cool.

5 Put the chestnut purée and icing sugar in a food processor and purée until smooth. Transfer the mixture to a bowl and stir in the brandy. Gently whisk in the cream until light and fluffy. Spread the filling over the roulade, leaving a 1 cm (½ inch) border. Roll it up from one short end to form a log. Serve dusted with icing sugar.

Pear, cardamom and sultana cake

Serves **12**
Preparation time **20 minutes**
Cooking time **1¼–1½ hours**

**125 g (4 oz) unsalted butter,
  softened**
**125 g (4 oz) soft light brown
  sugar**
2 eggs, lightly beaten
250 g (8 oz) self-raising flour
1 teaspoon ground cardamom
4 tablespoons milk
**500 g (1 lb) pears, peeled,
  cored and thinly sliced**
125 g (4 oz) sultanas
1 tablespoon clear honey

1 Put the butter and sugar in a bowl and beat together
until pale and light. Beat in the eggs, a little at a time, until
they are incorporated. Sift the flour and ground cardamom
together and fold them into the creamed mixture together
with the milk.

2 Reserve about one-third of the pear slices and roughly
chop the rest. Fold the chopped pears into the creamed
mixture with the sultanas.

3 Lightly oil and base-line a 1 kg (2 lb) loaf tin and spoon the
mixture into the tin. Smooth the surface, making a small
dip in the centre. Arrange the reserved pear slices down
the centre of the cake, pressing them in gently. Bake in a
preheated oven, 160°C (325°F), Gas Mark 3, for 1¼–1½ hours
or until a skewer inserted into the centre comes out clean.

4 Remove the cake from the oven and drizzle over the
honey. Leave to cool in the tin for 20 minutes and then
transfer to a wire rack to cool completely.

Apricot frangipane cake

Serves **10**
Preparation time **45 minutes**
Cooking time **about 50 minutes**

175 g (6 oz) **unsalted butter,
softened**
175 g (6 oz) **golden caster
sugar**
3 **eggs**
100 g (3½ oz) **self-raising flour**
175 g (6 oz) **ground almonds**
250 g (8 oz) **ready-to-eat dried
apricots, roughly chopped**
5 tablespoons **smooth
apricot jam**
2 tablespoons **brandy or
almond liqueur**
250 g (8 oz) **white almond
paste**
100 g (3½ oz) **whole sweet
almonds**
25 g (1 oz) **dried cranberries**
glacé icing, to decorate

1 Put the butter, sugar, eggs, flour and ground almonds in a bowl and beat the mixture until smooth and creamy. Stir in 150 g (5 oz) apricots.

2 Grease and line the base and sides of an 18 cm (7 inch) round cake tin. Grease the paper. Turn the mixture into the tin, level the surface and bake in a preheated oven, 160°C (325°F), Gas Mark 3, for 50 minutes or until just firm and a skewer inserted into the centre comes out clean. Transfer to a wire rack to cool.

3 Measure the circumference of the cake with a piece of string. Melt the jam with the liqueur in a small saucepan until smooth. Brush a little glaze over the top and sides of the cake. Roll out the almond paste and trim to a strip the length of the string and 1 cm (½ inch) deeper than the cake. Roll up the paste and unroll it around the sides of the cake.

4 Scatter with the remaining apricots, nuts and cranberries. Brush with the remaining glaze and scribble with icing.

Mango and coconut cake

Serves **10–12**
Preparation time **30 minutes**,
   plus cooling
Cooking time **30–35 minutes**

**50 g (2 oz) creamed coconut,
   chilled**
**150 g (5 oz) unsalted butter,
   softened**
150 g (5 oz) caster sugar
175 g (6 oz) self-raising flour
1 teaspoon baking powder
3 eggs
1 teaspoon vanilla extract

TO FINISH
75 g (3 oz) caster sugar
**finely grated rind and juice of
   3 limes**
5 tablespoons white rum
**300 ml (½ pint) extra thick
   double cream**
**2 medium mangoes,
   thinly sliced**
icing sugar, for dusting
**toasted coconut shavings,
   to decorate**

1 Finely grate the creamed coconut. Put the butter, sugar, flour, baking powder, eggs and vanilla extract in a bowl and beat until smooth and creamy. Stir in the coconut.

2 Grease and line the base and sides of a 23 cm (9 inch) round cake tin. Grease the paper. Turn the mixture into the tin, level the surface and bake in a preheated oven, 180°C (350°F), Gas Mark 4, for 25–30 minutes or until just firm. Transfer to a wire rack to cool.

3 Heat the sugar in a small saucepan with 100 ml (3½ fl oz) water until the sugar dissolves. Heat gently for 3 minutes, then leave to cool.

4 Cut the cake into 3 horizontal layers. Stir the lime rind, juice and rum into the syrup. Drizzle 3 tablespoonfuls of the liquid over each cake.

5 Whip the cream with the remaining syrup until it holds its shape. Sandwich the cakes with the mango slices and cream and dust the top generously with icing sugar. Scatter with toasted coconut shavings.

Coffee profiteroles with chocolate sauce

Makes **12 profiteroles**
Preparation time **20 minutes,**
   plus cooling
Cooking time **25 minutes**

CHOUX PASTRY
125 ml (4 fl oz) water
50 g (2 oz) chilled unsalted
   butter
65 g (2½ oz) plain flour, sifted
pinch of salt
2 eggs, lightly beaten

CHOCOLATE SAUCE
100 g (3½ oz) plain dark
   chocolate, chopped
50 g (2 oz) unsalted butter,
   diced
1 tablespoon golden syrup

COFFEE CREAM
300 ml (½ pint) double cream
2 tablespoons made espresso
   coffee, cooled
2 tablespoons Kahlua or
   Tia Maria

1   Make the pastry. Put the measurement water and butter in a small saucepan and heat gently until the butter has melted. Bring to the boil, remove the pan from the heat and immediately beat in the flour and salt until evenly combined.

2   Return the pan to a gentle heat and cook, stirring, until the mixture comes together and starts to leave the sides of the pan. Remove from the heat and beat in the eggs with a wooden spoon a little at a time, beating well after each addition until the egg is incorporated and the mixture is smooth and shiny.

3   Line a baking sheet with baking paper. Spoon the choux pastry dough into a piping bag fitted with a 2.5 cm (1 inch) plain nozzle and pipe 12 mounds on to the baking sheet, leaving plenty of space between each one. Bake in a preheated oven, 200°C (400°F), Gas Mark 6, for 20 minutes until puffed up and golden. Remove from the oven, cut a small slit in each one and return to the oven for a further 5 minutes to crisp up. Transfer to a wire rack to cool.

4   Make the chocolate sauce. Put the chocolate, butter and syrup in a small bowl set over a pan of gently simmering water and stir until melted. Leave to cool slightly.

5   Make the coffee cream. Whip the cream, coffee and liqueur together until stiff. Cut the choux buns almost in half and spoon or pipe the coffee cream into each one. Serve drizzled with the chocolate sauce.

Pistachio, lemon and polenta cake with rosewater syrup

Serves **6–8**
Preparation time **20 minutes**
Cooking time **about 1½ hours**

125 g (4 oz) plain flour
150 g (5 oz) polenta
200 g (7 oz) caster sugar
1 teaspoon baking powder
150 ml (¼ pint) olive oil
250 ml (8 fl oz) Greek yogurt
3 eggs
2 tablespoons rosewater
finely grated rind of 2 lemons
    and their juice
75 g (3 oz) pistachios, roughly
    chopped
Greek yogurt, to serve

ROSEWATER SYRUP
100 g (3½ oz) caster sugar
1 tablespoon rosewater
100 ml (3½ fl oz) water
rind of 1 lemon, pared in strips
    with a vegetable peeler

1 Combine the flour, polenta, sugar and baking powder in a large bowl. In a separate bowl whisk together the olive oil, yogurt, eggs and rosewater. Pour the yogurt mixture into the dry ingredients and beat with a wooden spoon until smooth. Stir in the lemon rind and juice and 50 g (2 oz) chopped pistachios.

2 Lightly oil and base-line a 23 cm (9 inch) springform cake tin, spoon the mixture into the tin, smooth the surface and bake in a preheated oven, 150°C (300°F), Gas Mark 2, for about 1½ hours or until golden and firm.

3 Meanwhile, make the syrup. Put all ingredients in a small saucepan and heat very gently, stirring occasionally, until the sugar has completely dissolved. Increase the heat slightly and leave to bubble gently, without stirring, for about 12 minutes until it forms a light syrup. Leave to cool, then shred the lemon peel very thinly.

4 Remove the cake from the oven and leave to cool for about 10 minutes. Scatter the cake with the remaining pistachios and the shredded lemon peel and pour half the cool syrup evenly over the top. Leave to cool completely still in the tin, then remove the cake and cut it into 6–8 wedges. Serve drizzled with the remaining syrup and a spoonful of Greek yogurt.

Chocolate truffle gâteau

Serves **12**
Preparation time **about 1 hour, plus chilling**
Cooking time **about 15 minutes**

2 eggs
50 g (2 oz) caster sugar
50 g (2 oz) plain flour

FILLING
450 ml (¾ pint) double cream
275 g (9 oz) milk chocolate, chopped
450 ml (¾ pint) Greek yogurt
275 g (9 oz) dark chocolate, chopped
cocoa powder, for dusting

CHOCOLATE MODELLING PASTE
190 g (6½ oz) plain dark or white chocolate, chopped
3¼ tablespoons golden syrup or liquid glucose

1 Make the modelling paste. Melt the chocolate in a heatproof bowl over a pan of simmering water. Remove from the heat and beat in the syrup or liquid glucose until the mixture forms a paste that leaves the sides of the bowl. Transfer to a plastic bag and chill for 30 minutes until firm.

2 Whisk the eggs and sugar in a heatproof bowl over a pan of simmering water until the whisk leaves a trail when lifted from the bowl. Remove from the heat and whisk until cool. Sift in the flour and fold with a large metal spoon.

3 Grease and base-line a 23 cm (9 inch) springform cake tin. Add the mixture and bake in a preheated oven, 190°C (375°F), Gas Mark 5, for 15 minutes until just firm to the touch. Cool on a wire rack. Clean the tin and re-line the sides. Halve the sponge horizontally. Place one half back in the tin.

4 Make the filling. Bring 225 ml (7½ fl oz) cream to the boil in a pan. Remove from the heat and stir in the milk chocolate until melted. Place in a bowl and stir in 225 ml (7½ fl oz) yogurt. Spoon the milk chocolate mixture over the sponge in the tin and spread until level. Chill until beginning to set.

5 Make another layer with the remaining 225 ml (7½ fl oz) cream and yogurt and the dark chocolate. Spread it over the milk chocolate; leave until just setting. Top with the second sponge and chill for 2–3 hours. Transfer the gâteau to a plate. Dredge the top of the gâteau with cocoa powder.

6 Cut the modelling paste into 4 pieces. Dust a surface with cocoa powder. Roll the 4 pieces thinly into 12 cm (5 inch) rounds. Cut each round in half. Press the curved edge of each semicircle to make it wavy. Arrange the 8 pieces around the gâteau with the straight edges on the plate.

Chocolate cappuccino slice

Serves **10**
Preparation time **about 1 hour,
  plus cooling**
Cooking time **about 15 minutes**

3 eggs
75 g (3 oz) caster sugar
75 g (3 oz) plain flour
1 tablespoon finely ground
  espresso coffee

**CREME PATISSIERE
  (CONFECTIONERS' CUSTARD)**
1 tablespoon cornflour
2 egg yolks
75 g (3 oz) caster sugar
1 tablespoon finely ground
  espresso coffee
15 g (½ oz) cocoa powder
450 ml (¾ pint) milk
4 tablespoons Kahlua or other
  coffee-flavoured liqueur

TO DECORATE
175 g (6 oz) plain dark or milk
  chocolate, chopped
300 ml (½ pint) double cream
chocolate curls

1 Whisk the eggs and sugar in a large heatproof bowl over a pan of simmering water until the mixture leaves a trail when the whisk is lifted. Remove from the heat and whisk until cool. Sift in the flour and coffee and fold in with a metal spoon.

2 Grease and line a 23 x 33 cm (9 x 13 inch) Swiss roll tin and turn the mixture into the tin, easing it into the corners. Bake in a preheated oven, 200°C (400°F), Gas Mark 6, for about 12 minutes until just firm to the touch.

3 Sprinkle greaseproof paper with sugar and invert the sponge on to it. Remove the tin, peel away the lining; let cool.

4 Make the crème pâtissière. Mix the cornflour, egg yolks, sugar, espresso, cocoa powder and a little milk. Boil the rest of the milk and pour over the egg mixture, whisking well. Return the mixture to the pan and boil, whisking until thickened. Put in a bowl, cover with greaseproof. Let cool.

5 Cut the sponge widthways into 3 rectangles. Put 1 layer on a plate. Beat the Kahlua into the custard. Spread one-third over the sponge. Top with a second sponge, more custard, then the third sponge. Cover the top and sides with custard.

6 Make the decoration. Melt the chocolate in a heatproof bowl over a pan of simmering water, stirring occasionally. Cut a strip of greaseproof paper 8.5 cm (3½ inches) wide and 1 cm (½ inch) longer than the cake's circumference. Spread the melted chocolate down the strip, taking the chocolate to one long edge and shaping the other long edge into a wavy pattern. Leave 1 cm (½ inch) free at one end. Lift the strip and wrap it around the cake. Chill for about 10 minutes to set. Peel away the paper. Whip the cream into peaks and pile on the sponge. Top with chocolate curls.

Strawberry shortcake with elderflower cream

Makes **8 cakes**
Preparation time **20 minutes,**
  plus cooling
Cooking time **10–15 minutes**

250 g (8 oz) self-raising flour
2 teaspoons baking powder
75 g (3 oz) unsalted butter,
  diced
40 g (1½ oz) caster sugar
1 egg, lightly beaten
2–3 tablespoons milk
15 g (½ oz) unsalted butter,
  melted
250 g (8 oz) strawberries,
  hulled and sliced
icing sugar, to dust

ELDERFLOWER CREAM
300 ml (½ pint) double cream
2 tablespoons elderflower
  syrup

1 Sift the flour and baking powder into a bowl, rub in the butter, stir in the sugar and then gradually work in the egg and milk to form a soft dough. Alternatively, sift the flour and baking powder into the bowl of a food processor and add the butter. Pulse briefly until the mixture resembles breadcrumbs. Stir in the sugar. Add the egg and milk and process until the mixture comes together to form a dough.

2 Transfer the dough to a lightly floured surface and roll it out to 1 cm (½ inch) thick. Use an 8 cm (3 inch) round cutter to stamp out 8 rounds. Place the rounds on a large, lightly oiled baking sheet and brush each with a little melted butter. Bake in a preheated oven, 200°C (400°F), Gas Mark 6, for 10–15 minutes until risen and golden. Remove from the oven and transfer to a wire rack to cool. While they are still warm carefully split each cake in half horizontally and return to the wire rack until cold.

3 Make the elderflower cream. Put the cream and elderflower syrup in a bowl and whisk until thickened. Spread the cream over the base of each cake, top with strawberries and the cake lids. Serve dusted with icing sugar.

Easter nest torte

Serves 12
Preparation time **30 minutes,**
  plus standing and chilling
Cooking time **30 minutes**

50 g (2 oz) self-raising flour
½ teaspoon baking powder
40 g (1½ oz) cocoa powder
125 g (4 oz) unsalted butter,
  soften
125 g (4 oz) caster sugar
2 eggs
4 tablespoons orange-
  flavoured liqueur or
  orange juice
75 g (3 oz) milk chocolate,
  broken into pieces

FILLING
2 teaspoons powdered
  gelatine
2 tablespoons cold water
3 egg yolks
50 g (2 oz) caster sugar
1 teaspoon cornflour
300 ml (½ pint) milk
200 g (7 oz) milk chocolate,
  chopped
300 ml (½ pint) whipping
  cream

TO DECORATE
150 g (5 oz) milk chocolate at
  room temperature
small chocolate eggs

1 Sift the flour, baking powder and cocoa powder into a bowl. Whisk in the butter, sugar and eggs until creamy. Grease and base-line a 23 cm (9 inch) springform cake tin. Add the mixture, level the surface and bake in a preheated oven, 150°C (300°F), Gas Mark 2, for 20–25 minutes. Cool on a wire rack. Move to a plate and drizzle with liqueur or juice.

2 Cut a strip of greaseproof paper 6 cm (2½ inches) deep and 1 cm (½ inch) longer than the cake's circumference. Melt the chocolate and spoon it along the strip, spreading it to the edge on one side and making a wavy line on the other, about 2 cm (¾ inch) from the edge. Leave 1 cm (½ inch) free at one end. Set aside for 15 minutes, then secure the paper strip around the sponge so the straight chocolate edge rests on the plate and the ends of the strip just meet. Chill.

3 Make the filling. Sprinkle the gelatine over the top of the measurement water and allow to soften. Beat the egg yolks, sugar, cornflour and a little milk. Bring the rest of the milk to the boil. Pour it over the egg mixture, whisking well. Return the mixture to the pan and cook gently, stirring, until thickened.

4 Remove from the heat and stir in the gelatine until dissolved. Add the chopped chocolate to the milk and egg mixture and leave to melt. Stir until smooth, then turn into a bowl, cover with greaseproof paper, allow to cool until just beginning to thicken, then remove the paper.

5 Whip the cream to soft peaks; fold into the chocolate mixture. Place in the chocolate mould on the sponge; level the surface. Chill until set. Remove the greaseproof paper.

6 Slice the milk chocolate into long, thin shards. Lay them on the cake in a nest with the eggs. Chill until ready to serve.

Marbled espresso and vanilla cake

Serves **8–10**
Preparation time **25 minutes,**
   plus chilling
Cooking time **50 minutes**

1 tablespoon instant espresso
   coffee
175 g (6 oz) unsalted butter,
   softened
175 g (6 oz) caster sugar
3 eggs
200 g (7 oz) self-raising flour
½ teaspoon baking powder
1 teaspoon vanilla extract
unsweetened cocoa powder,
   for dusting

VANILLA MAPLE BUTTER
125 g (4 oz) unsalted butter,
   softened
1½ teaspoons vanilla bean
   paste
2 tablespoons icing sugar
175 g (6 oz) pure maple syrup

1   Make the vanilla maple butter. Put the butter, vanilla bean paste and sugar in a small bowl and beat together until the ingredients are combined. Gradually blend in the maple syrup, a little at a time, until the mixture is soft and smooth. Transfer to a small serving dish, cover and chill until required. (The butter may be kept in the refrigerator for up to 1 week.)

2   Mix the coffee with 1 tablespoon hot water. Put the butter, sugar, eggs, flour and baking powder in a separate bowl and beat for 1–2 minutes until pale and creamy. Spoon half the mixture into a separate bowl. Add the vanilla extract to one bowl and the coffee to the other.

3   Grease and base-line a 20 cm (8 inch) springform cake tin. Put heaped teaspoonfuls of the coffee mixture in the tin, spacing them well apart and using about half the mixture. Spoon half the vanilla mixture into the gaps over the base of the pan. Layer with the remaining mixtures, keeping the flavours separate if possible, then level the surface. Lightly swirl a knife through the mixtures to marble them together but do not overmix, or the colours and flavours will merge.

4   Bake in a preheated oven, 180°C (350°F), Gas Mark 4, for about 50 minutes or until the cake is firm to the touch. Transfer to a wire rack to cool.

5   Swirl the top of the cake with the maple butter and serve dusted with a little cocoa powder.

Simnel cake

Serves **10**
Preparation time **25 minutes**
Cooking time **3 hours**

175 g (6 oz) unsalted butter
175 g (6 oz) caster sugar
3 large eggs, lightly beaten
175 g (6 oz) plain flour
1 teaspoon ground cinnamon
1 teaspoon grated nutmeg
475 g (15 oz) currants
125 g (4 oz) sultanas
50 g (2 oz) chopped candied
** peel**
1–2 tablespoons milk
500 g (1 lb) marzipan
3–4 tablespoons apricot jam
1 egg, beaten, for glazing

1 Cream together the butter and sugar and beat in the eggs a tablespoon at a time, mixing well between each addition. Sift the flour with the spices and fold this in, followed by the dried fruit. Mix to a soft consistency with a little milk.

2 Grease and line an 18 cm (7 inch) round cake tin. Put half the mixture into the tin and level it.

3 Divide the marzipan into 3 pieces and roll out one-third into a round slightly smaller than the tin. Pinch the edges so the marzipan does not crack and lay it over the cake mixture. Put the other half of the cake mixture on top and level it. Tie a band of brown paper round the outside of the pan to come 5 cm (2 inches) above it to protect the top of the cake during baking. Bake in a preheated oven, 160°C (325°F), Gas Mark 3, for 1 hour. Reduce the temperature to 250°C (300°F), Gas Mark 2, and cook for a further 2 hours or until the cake is firm to the touch. Allow to cool in the tin before removing the lining paper and transferring the cake to a wire rack to cool.

4 Heat the jam and push through a sieve if lumpy. Roll out a reserved piece of marzipan into a round for the cake top. Brush the apricot glaze over the cake and press on the marzipan. Pinch the edges into flutes.

5 Flatten the remaining marzipan, divide it into 11 equal pieces and roll each into a small ball. Brush the top and sides of the marzipan on the cake with beaten egg. Press on the balls round the edge of the cake. Glaze with beaten egg, then brown under a hot grill. When the cake is cool, it can be wrapped in foil and stored for at least 2 weeks.

White chocolate and raspberry puffs

Serves **6**
Preparation time **40 minutes,**
   plus chilling
Cooking time **15 minutes**

150 g (5 oz) raspberries
icing sugar, to dust

PUFF PASTRY
125 g (4 oz) plain flour, sifted
½ teaspoon salt
125 g (4 oz) chilled unsalted
   butter
½ tablespoon lemon juice
50–75 ml (2–3 fl oz) cold water

WHITE CHOCOLATE CREAM
200 ml (7 fl oz) single cream
½ vanilla pod
200 g (7 oz) white chocolate,
   chopped

1 Make the pastry. Put the flour and salt in a bowl and rub in 25 g (1 oz) of the butter until the mixture resembles bread-crumbs. Make a well in the centre. Add the juice and water. Slowly work to form a soft dough. Put the rest of the butter between sheets of clingfilm. Roll to an 8 cm (3 inch) square.

2 Roll out the dough on a lightly floured surface to a 15 cm (6 inch) square. Put the butter diagonally in the centre of the dough. Fold the exposed dough over the butter, pressing down the seams to enclose it. Wrap and chill for 20 minutes.

3 Roll out the dough on a lightly floured surface to 10–20 cm (4–8 inches). Fold the top third down toward the centre of the dough and the bottom third up over the top. Press down the edges with the rolling pin. Wrap and chill for 15 minutes.

4 Turn the dough through 90° so that the narrow end faces you. Roll, fold and chill for a further 15 minutes. Repeat the turning, rolling and folding process a further 3 times.

5 Roll out the pastry dough on a lightly floured surface to a rectangle 2 mm (⅛ inch) thick. Cut it into 6 rectangles, each 7 x 12 cm (3 x 5 inches). Put on a baking sheet and chill for 30 minutes. Bake in a preheated oven, 200°C (400°F), Gas Mark 6, for 15 minutes until the pastry is puffed. Cool on a rack.

6 Make the chocolate cream. Gently bring the cream and vanilla pod to the boil. Remove from the heat and scrape the seeds from the vanilla pod into the cream. Immediately stir in the chocolate and continue stirring until it has melted. Cool, chill for 1 hour until firm and then whisk until stiff.

7 Split the pastries in half crossways and fill with chocolate cream and raspberries. Serve dusted with icing sugar.

Index

Acknowledgements

Executive Editor: Nicky Hill

Editor: Leanne Bryan

Design Manager: Tokiko Morishima

Designer: Ginny Zeal

Picture Researcher: Taura Riley

Production Controller: Nosheen Shan

Picture acknowledgements

© Octopus Publishing Group Limited/Stephen Conroy 18,
81, 90–91, 120; /Vanessa Davies 1, 25, 29, 34, 52, 79, 83; /Gus
Filgate 30, 115; /David Jordan 44; /William Lingwood 41, 88; /
Lis Parsons 12–13, 27, 49, 54–55, 71, 74, 102; /William Reavell
28; /Gareth Sambidge 7, 15, 16, 23, 56–57, 66–67, 87, 93; /Ian
Wallace 20, 33, 37, 60–61, 84–85, 95, 101, 104–105, 107, 109,
119, 125; /Phillip Webb 38–39.